HALLOWEEN SCHOOL PARTIES

What Do I Do?™

All of the ideas in this book can be adapted to parties outside of school.

Wilhelminia Ripple

Illustrated By Heather Anderson

Halloween School Parties:

Halloween School Parties: What Do I Do?™ Author Wilhelminia Ripple

Printed and bound in the United States of America.

First Edition 1996
Printing 10 9 8 7 6 5 4 3 2

Library of Congress Catalog Card Number: 96-92239

ISBN: 0-9649939-8-8

Summary: Parent/Teacher guide includes eight themes, games, crafts/favors, treats, parent costumes, illustrations, helpful hints. Includes index
1. Holiday 2. How-to

To order (only):
1-888-738-1733

Oakbrook Publishing House
P.O. Box 2463
Littleton, Colorado 80161-2463
(303) 738-1733
FAX: (303) 797-1995

Attention Organizations: Quantity discounts are available for bulk purchases. For information please call or write to the above (Oakbrook Publishing House).

This Book is
Happily Dedicated:

To my husband Mark
(his love helped make this book happen)

and

To my children Mark, Nick, and Michelle
(for their help and understanding)

and

To my Mom Dolores
(who has always been creative, and inspired me)

and

To my Dad Samuel
(Whom I wish could be here)

and

To all who believed in me!

Acknowledgments

Thank you to my family and friends who helped me in so many ways. Laurie Bacheller, Marilyn Degner, Lynn Finger, Jeff, Pam, & Donna Kortman, Linda Myers, and Carol Sue Kruise, *Author of Learning through Literature available from Permabound Books and Those Bloomin' Books from Libraries Unlimited.*

Special thanks to Julie Krohn, Nancy Ecker, and Joanne Hill who helped with the editing. And to Joanne, for being my first room mother that I ever talked with and who is now a special friend. Special thanks to Paula Farney for her testimonial, Karen Timm poet/author for writing the Halloween poem, and Pam Chapman for her special handwriting. Thanks also to all of the room parents that I have worked with throughout the years, and all of the children and teachers in classes where I was the room parent.

Special thanks to all the children and adults who allowed me to interview them: Chelsea & Steve Alles, Debby Baldwin, Beth Bear, Sandy Boyd, Kim Davis, Christie, Jill & Katie Day, Nancy Ecker, Paula Garb, Jessica Hoskins, Joanne Hill, Kelly Hill, Janet Isaacs, Barb Johnson, Allison, Lynne & Megan Knight, Pamela Kortman, David & Jonathan Krohn, Beckee, Rachel & Timothy Laurie, Becky Leon, Jill Linden, Ginny Lyons, Megan Lyons, Melissa Lyons, Stephanie Lyons, Diana Mason, Laurie McCaslin, Debbie Morey, Derek, Kali & Tammy O'Neil, Faunie Parker, Mark, Nick & Michelle Ripple, Gloria Schwiesow, Karen Simpson, Kari, Kathy & Kori Talbott, Jennifer Thomsen, Nancy Werner, and Joy Wilson.

Thank you to Kappie Originals, Ltd., 801 East Street, Frederick, MD 21701, for their permission to include the following magnets from their book *Magnificent Magnets* Book 216: bat, ghost, pumpkin, and spider; and also Coney Cousin Bat and Halloween Cat from their book *Coney Cousins* Book 212.

Thank you to the following who were patient in working with me:
     Editor - Alicia Fields Rudnicki
     Illustrator - Heather Anderson
     Cover Designer - Bobbi Shupe of E.P. Puffin & Company
     Graphic Artists - Eric & Erika at Graphics Plus

And if I have forgotten you "Thank You!"

About the Author

Wilhelminia "Willie" Ripple was encouraged to write this book because of the many children, parents, and teachers who have enjoyed the school parties that she has coordinated. She has eight years of experience in collecting and creating Halloween party ideas. As a mother of school-age children, Willie is actively involved in assorted school events. She has had fun coordinating the school carnival, the school memory book, and party training sessions for parents. Her creativity doesn't stop there. Willie, also a hairdresser, now lives in Colorado with her husband, Mark, and three children.

IV

Table of Contents

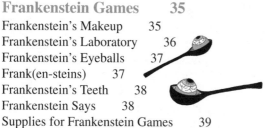

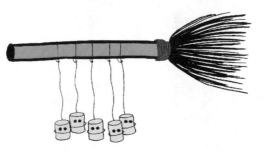

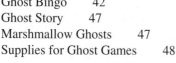

Chapter 3. Crafts & Favors 79

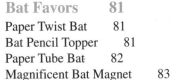

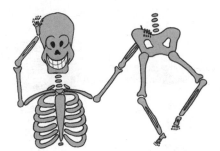

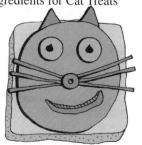

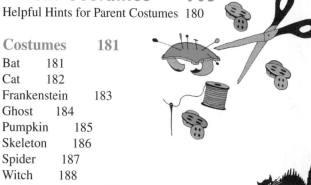

The Halloween Party

by Karen Timm

The parents got together early one night
To plan a party for their children's delight
They wanted some games, costumes and eats,
But needed a plan to go with their treats.

Ann said witches and scary black cats.
Joe liked spiders and vampire bats.
Skeletons and ghosts, Rosemary said.
John wanted Frankenstein, arose from the dead.

Eenie, meenie, miny, moe
What should it be?
Which way should they go?

Julie said, wait, it's all in here!
This book makes everything very clear.
It's called Halloween School Parties: What Do I Do?™
With ideas and easy instructions for you.

It has games like "Bat Toss" and "Black Cat Eyes,"
And spider web favors for the childrens' surprise.
With skeleton straw games and clothespin bats,
And creepy crawling spiders and mini witch hats.

In one short night they had figured it out,
Each parent knew what to do without doubt.
With tricks and treats and costumes so clever,
They had easily planned the best party ever.

Introduction

How to use this Book

Halloween School Parties: What Do I Do?™ will supply you with plenty of tricks, treats, and tips to help you prepare for classroom Halloween parties for kindergarten through sixth grade. These ideas can also be adapted to Halloween parties outside of school. This book answers concerns about organizing class parties and contains six "how-to" chapters on games, crafts and favors, treats, drinks, and parent costumes — all designed to help you plan your party with ease.

If you enjoy theme parties, there are eight to choose from in this book: Bats, Cats, Frankenstein, Ghosts, Pumpkins, Skeletons, Spiders, and Witches. For example, the chapter on games suggests a variety of fun activities to fit each theme. Go through each chapter and pick what you'd like to use; feel free to combine ideas from different themes. Within minutes your party will be planned: no more fussing, no more headaches. It couldn't be easier.

After choosing a theme or combination of themes, decide how many games you will have time for during your party. Most of the games in this book can be played in five minutes. Choose your games based on the theme(s) you have chosen. Feel free to adapt the materials in this book to fit your needs. You may not want to make any of the crafts and may prefer store-bought favors. This is certainly alright, especially if you are short on time. Now move on to the treat and drink chapters looking for refreshments to match your chosen theme(s). Plan on serving two treats. One is not enough.

Each drink recipe will provide 28 one-cup servings, 37 three-quarter cup servings or 56 half-cup servings. Typically, fifth and sixth graders will drink one cup or more. Second, third, and fourth graders need a three-quarter cup serving whereas half a cup is plenty for kindergartners and first graders. Are you looking at these figures thinking that your child could drink more? I agree, they can, but my experience as a classroom party planner has taught me that most children don't. They are just too busy with all of the excitement that a lot of drinks go into the trash. However, if it is a very hot day, plan larger serving sizes. Don't forget that the parent volunteers attending the party and the classroom teacher will want to have some drinks as well.

One fun way to make your party a success is for the parent volunteers to dress in costumes according to the theme(s) you have chosen. The chapter on parent costumes offers a number of ideas involving minimal work. A popular plan for a school Halloween party is to divide into four themes. Choose one game from each of the four different themes. Set up four stations for these games in various parts of the classroom so that students can take turns circulating from one activity to the next. To split the class into groups, make nametags that coordinate with the themes. These can be made out of construction paper or felt. Mix all of them into a cauldron-type container (you may be able to find these in grocery, discount, and craft stores), then have the kids draw a tag out. The tags are pinned or taped to their clothing and signify what station each student will start at.

The themes in this book are meant to make things easy for you. Use them in any combination you would like. Remember, "no more fussing, no more headaches. It couldn't be easier."

Key to Symbols Used Throughout this Book

Knowledge Symbol
Educational facts relating to themes to share with the children.

Favorite Symbol
Don't miss this game (craft, treat, etc.)

Messy Symbol
Sure to cause dirty hands or faces: have paper towels ready.

Supply Symbol
Complete list of needed items, *for each game/list, treat, etc.*

Tombstone Symbol
Easy to copy, complete list of all ingredients/supplies needed for *each section.*

CHAPTER ONE

The What, Why, and How of Room Parenting.

Halloween School Parties:

What value do you see in being a room parent?

Laurie McCaslin:
"I had a blast! My daughters love it when I'm involved. I see great value in being a room parent and being a party planner is a fun way to be involved."

Lynn Knight:
"It helps to instill in my children the importance of their education."

Tammy O'Neil:
"Its a good way to spend extra time with my children and see them in a classroom setting."

Barb Johnson:
"It improves your organizational skills."

What is a Room Parent?

There are many definitions for the term "room parent." I guess the technical definition is "someone who assists the teacher in various ways." As a room parent you might help the teacher in the classroom with cutting, pasting, making copies, organizing book orders, assisting on field trips, reading stories, baking, etc. The list varies at each school.

The purpose of this book is to help the room parent in another area that is often their responsibility — classroom party planning. At my childrens' school some room parents who wanted only to help with school parties were confused by the title "room parents," so we decided to call these parents "party planners." Therefore, our party planners' only purpose is to plan parties for the school year and it is our room parents' responsibility to help the teacher in other ways. But, for the sake of not confusing you, throughout this book the title "room parents" will be used instead of "party planners" since the former is more widely accepted. I also use the word "parent" even though a room parent may be a grandparent, uncle, aunt, friend, neighbor or community member.

What is a Room Party?

A room party is held at school during school time. Many schools hold these parties the last hour of the day. An example of an exception would be a morning kindergarten class which would hold their party in the morning. Each class has its own party, which is usually held in its classroom. A typical party, consists of playing games and having refreshments as well as taking home favors and/or making a craft. The party is given by parents, not the teacher or school. Parties typically last about one hour or less. Usually the teacher stays for the party.

This book focuses on Halloween parties for school. However, other common parties at schools can be a Christmas or winter party, a Valentine's Day party, and a Easter or spring party. Many schools hold only two school wide holiday parties a year.

How Do You Become a Room Parent?

Parents who are new to a school, because of moving or because their oldest child has just entered kindergarten, should check to see what's expected of them when they sign up to be a room parent. You can usually sign up at back-to-school night or curriculum night at the beginning of the school year. Some schools might also send home a volunteer sign-up package during the first few weeks of school. Every school will be different, so check with your child's teacher. If you only want to help with a specific event such as the Halloween party, but your school's room parents do more, then write that on the sign-up sheet. But please don't hesitate to volunteer even if work or other circumstances limit what you can do.

Once everyone signs up, a head room parent needs to be chosen. Your teacher, room parent coordinator, or Parent Teacher Organization (PTO) might do the choosing. (In some schools, the parent-teacher support group is called PTA — Parent Teacher Association — or PTSA — Parent Teacher Student Association— or PA — Parent Association. Throughout this book we will use the term PTO.) Sometimes there are two or three parents for the same class who would like to be the head room parent; sometimes there is nobody. Some schools ask several parents to work together or assign one parent to be head room parent for one party and another to handle the other party. This way works great!

There can never be too many room parents; well, almost never. Kindergarten classes can have an overwhelming number of room parents. But it sure does make for less work for everyone and a better party for the kids.

Note: If you can't attend a classroom party or help plan the event, why not offer to donate materials or bake goodies? Keep in mind that your child is invited to the party.

Why Should You Be a Room Parent?

- Because you are needed!
- It's one more step in the right direction to being a better parent.
- Not only do your children appreciate you, but the teacher, the school, and the other children do also.
- Children learn what they see. It's important for our kids to see us helping out.
- Being around children at school will make you feel young again.
- It's a great opportunity to make friends.
- You gain valuable experience from teamwork.
- It keeps you in tune with how your child acts in class.
- Kids whose parents volunteer at school tend to do better overall.
- You might revive some lost creativity.

What is a Head Room Parent?

Each class usually has a head room parent whose purpose is to serve as a contact person that can be reached by other room parents, teachers, and the PTO. The head parent job can include but is not limited to:

1. Calling other class room parents to plan the party.

2. Communicating with the teacher, PTO, school administration, etc.

3. Collecting and distributing class party money.

4. Turning in a record of volunteer hours to the PTO or the school district.

Your school will let you know what your responsibilities are.

Help for the Head Room Parent

You have been selected as head room parent for your child's class. Congratulations.

Here are some helpful tips:

At least three weeks before the party call and meet with your other room parents (who could be moms, dads, grandmas, grandpas, aunts, uncles, and legal guardians—don't refuse anybody or any help). Some room parents feel more comfortable starting four weeks ahead. Caution: Assignments given to some helpers can get lost or forgotten if you start too soon. But also keep in mind that a lot of room parents get nervous if not called at least two weeks before the party. What might work better for early planners would be to call room parents at four weeks but to schedule a meeting at three weeks.

Why should you be a room parent?

Jill Linden:
"It's an easy way to be involved in your child's school and it doesn"t take an enormous amount of time."

Steve Alles:
"Because you can have an effect on the learning process and you can actually spend some time with your child during the day."

Nancy Werner:
"Because of guilt. A parent want's to do so much in the school with their child and sometimes are not able to do so."

What did you enjoy the most about being a head room parent?

Jennifer Thomsen:
"Finding fun new games to play with the kids."

Joy Wilson:
"The parties and the parents that helped and the friends I have made."

Beckee Laurie:
"Seeing how much fun the kids have."

Halloween School Parties:

What value do you see in being a room Parent?

Jill Day:
"I like it because teachers think you're wonderful, and it's fun. Moms and kids just wanna have fun!"

Becky Leon:
"Kids are always so appreciative of your efforts and they reflect that in their smiling faces. The elementary years are so rewarding, but they pass much too quickly. Being a room parent allows you to interact with the kids and to play an active role during those fleeting years.

Debbie Morey:
"My older kids look back at me being at school and appreciate me being there and that's really rewarding."

Before your scheduled meeting, communicate with the classroom teacher. Communicating could mean talking on the phone, writing a note, or catching the teacher at a break time such as recess, lunch, or after school. I have found that teachers prefer a note because they can answer my questions right on that paper, then send it back to me. I keep the note to refer back to.

If you are new to your child's school, an experienced parent can tell you how your teacher prefers to be contacted. Some teachers will tell you at curriculum night or back-to-school night. Allow a week for the teacher to return your note. Most return it in a day, but you may have to wait longer and even remind some teachers that they never answered.

Here are some questions for the teacher that will help you plan your party:

1. How many children are in the class? How many boys? How many girls?

2. Are there any new students? (This is important if you had a previous count from the beginning of the year.)

3. Does anybody, including the teacher, have food allergies? This is very important!

4. Are there any children with physical disabilities?

5. Can the desks and chairs be rearranged?

6. Do you prefer the children to eat when the party first starts or after playing games?

7. Do you have any preferences for games, food, favors, crafts, etc.?

8. How do you like to handle younger siblings coming to the party?

9. What time should the party start and end? (This information might be given to you by the room parent coordinator.)

10. Is it okay to set up in the room before the party begins? If your school has a Halloween parade prior to the party, add these questions to your list:

11. Would you like to have parents help the children get into their costumes? (Teachers of younger grades love the help.)

12. How long will the parade last?

13. Can we set up for the party while the kids are parading?

Setting up while the parade is going on can work well. The only problem is that the room parents want to watch the parade and take pictures. To avoid this bring in the supplies earlier that day — preferably in the morning before class begins, or at recess, at lunch, or the day before the party. Once the supplies are in the room, setting them up in the right areas usually should take no more than five minutes. Parents I work with usually accomplish set-up as the children leave for the parade, so we still have time to watch the parade, take pictures, and ooh and ah about our kids.

Whatever method you use, avoid interrupting the class. No matter how quiet you are, the kids will stop what they are doing and wave or say hi! They are curious and want to know what's going on. Some teachers do not appreciate this distraction. Here is one final question to ask teachers of older children (grades 5 and 6) wishing to combine classes for a huge party: Is it okay to combine other classes from the same level for one huge party in the gym, such as a haunted house?

The next step after calling all your room parents and scheduling a meeting, is to jot down a few notes or just think about what the meeting should cover. This way you can get down to business when the time comes. An hour or more can go by very fast without you ever covering your agenda. This is irritating for many parents who are on a tight schedule. By making it known what time the meeting will end you can help keep it on track. What works well is to give a handout sheet such as the room parents assignment list which appears on page 20. Everyone can make their own notes page 21 and remember, at a later date, what they are responsible for.

It is fun to make a little party out of this first planning meeting. I like to serve refreshments, usually something simple like cookies and punch. If you serve your treats with Halloween paper goods, it helps get the parents in the party mood. They will be surprised and pleased by your extra touches.

As a head room parent you may also opt for a meeting at a restaurant or at school to avoid serving refreshments and cleaning your house. The meeting will seem more business-like. If you choose to meet at school, ask your PTO or school office where you can meet and whether your scheduled meeting time is okay in that location. Remember to keep down the noise and encourage younger children not to run around if your meeting is held at school.

When the meeting is at your house, it helps not to seat children at the table where you will be working. Plan an area where any young visitors can play within sight of their parents. Put toys out or put a video into the VCR. A meeting without children would be ideal but isn't always possible. My experience has shown me that a two-hour meeting is best because there will always be problems such as people arriving late or leaving early. *Caution:* Don't assume all is okay when you don't hear from your parent volunteers, only assume all is okay when you verify with them. Call them a few days before the party (and the night before if you need to) to see if they have done what they said they would.

Class Party Money.

At most schools money is collected from each student to be used for class parties. This is usually done at the beginning of the school year. Collections can vary from $2 to $10 for the school year. That amount is divided between the number of parties. For example, at a school where there are two parties — Halloween and Valentines Day — $2 might be collected from each student ($1 per student for each party). If a class has 25 students they would col-

lect $50 in party money if each student's family pays. Each school handles the collection and distribution of the money the way it thinks best.

Some schools collect the money by way of the classroom teachers who turn it in to the school office. Then it is given to the PTO, which distributes the money to the head room parents. Money for the Halloween party usually is given out in September whereas January is the usual time to distribute money for the Valentine's Day party. There are two ways in which PTOs generally handle party money. First, PTO may choose not to distribute the money to head room parents but to buy bulk favors, drinks, and napkins, etc., for the whole school. This may

How does your school handle party money?

Joanne Hill:
"Due to a move, I have dealt with two elementary schools. Each school asks that each child donate $1.00 per party. At our first school, parent's usually agreed to donate items. This allowed us to save the money that we collected for an end of the year party or teacher gift. My experience so far at the new school has been a little different. The mothers save their receipts and are reimbursed for their party expenses."

Canton, Ohio

Diana Mason:
"As far as the money goes, room mom's donate all needed items. No money is collected for parties."
North Platte, Nebraska

15

Halloween School Parties:

How does your school handle party money?

Janet Isacas:
"Be organized, make sure class party money covers all expenses. Know who's bringing what and what you are lacking. Call everyone the night before."
Littleton, Colorado

Nancy Ecker:
"The school collects $10.00 at the begining of the school year which is split between the Halloween and Valentines party. Room parents buy individual favors for each student in the class. They also buy supplies for games to participate in the class. It also covers cakes, drinks, paper products and other items."
San Ramon, California

be done to try to treat all classes equally. Room parents would still plan all the games, crafts, activities, and food for their individual classrooms, but would have no class money to work with. In this situation, you need to have things donated. Some parents feel that they donate enough through school fund raisers and the giving of their time. So, be as careful as possible when asking for donations.

Second, PTO may collect the money from all the classes and divide that amount per student to obtain a per-student figure. For example, if you have 450 students and should receive $2 per student you should have $900. But if all the money hasn't been collected the per-student figure will be less than $2. Let's say you only received $810; you would still divide that amount by 450 students. This would give you a $1.80 per student figure to divide between two parties — or $.90 per student per party. You would then multiply $.90 times the number of students in each class to determine the total amount given to each classroom per party. For example, if there are twenty students in a class, then it would receive $18 for the Halloween party and the same amount for the Valentine's Day party. This per-student method of allocating party money may vary somewhat from school to school. At some schools, for example, if there is a shortfall, PTO may choose to make up the difference in order to ensure $2 per student. Any questions regarding party money should be directed to the proper source. This might be the principal or the PTO. Check with your child's teacher.

Quick Tips for the Room Parent Coordinator/Chairperson

1. Plan a meeting for room parents (especially head room parents) a month before the Halloween party. Have example tables with plently of ideas for crafts/favors and treats. Room parents find this especially helpful . Hand out any party information and money at this time. Our school found it helpful to have head room parents sign for the money .

2. Call all head room mothers about a week before the party. Ask them to tell you a little about their party. This is a time a lot of room parents asked for help with planning their party (especially games). I usually suggested easy games. They helped the most because they hadn't planned any yet and time was running out. I also asked how they were doing with the budget.

3. Give the head room parent the party report form on page 19 to fill out. It is quite helpful for future uses.

Helpful Hints for Room Parents

1. Physical education teachers, music teachers, librarians, secretaries, custodians, and the principal are usually forgotten as potential classroom helpers at party time. They are good resources for you if you do not have enough parent volunteer help for the day. You can even plan extra treats/drinks for them. (If you have a lot of extra refreshments, you may want to set them in the teachers' lounge for everyone to enjoy.)

2. For easier cleanup, bring a large plastic garbage bag to the party. The bag will eliminate overflowing trash cans, and the custodians will love you. It also helps to have a roll of paper towels or a sponge for spills, which we know will happen.

3. Do you have any extra children's costumes? Bring them along because they might come in handy for children who have forgotten or don't have costumes.

4. A Halloween activity done on paper, such as a crossword puzzle, works well as a back-up activity for children who run out of things to do or who are waiting to take turns at a particular game. (Try not to have too much waiting time. Kids are ready to go.)

5. Kids can draw numbers or straws to decide who starts or finishes a game.

6. Give prizes to all the kids.

7. The children will probably be in costumes during the party, so beware of any difficulties this may create when playing the games.

8. If trying a new game, practice it first at home, but try to keep it a secret from your child who will be attending the party.

9. Dividing the class into smaller groups works best. For older grades, groups of three work well if you want to do a relay race and have three teams compete one at a time. Dividing the class into boys versus girls works great in fourth through sixth grades.

10. As previously mentioned in the introduction, a good way to divide the kids into rotating groups is to give them tags based on the party's combination of themes. I have made the ghost, pumpkin, bat, and witch magnets described in chapter 3 for use as tags. I put them all in a pretend witch's cauldron, mixed them up, and let the kids reach in to choose one to pin on their costume like a name tag. The magnets make nice favors to take home. Another great idea for dividing into groups is to give the students name tags that are Halloween shapes cut out of construction paper. Or try using the same shape (for example, bats) but on different colors of paper.

11. Give name tags to all the room parents as well as the children. For younger grades it works well to write "Michelle's mom," and "Nick's dad" on the tags. For older grades, it is appropriate to write out the parent's last name (for example, "Mrs. Ripple").

Do you have any tips for room parents?

Kathy Talbot:
"Be prepared. make sure you have all of your supplies in the car. Double Check! Leave plenty of time for set up so you're not stressed."

Faunie Parker:
1. *Plan more activities than you think you'll need*

2. *Have some healthy snacks*

3. *Face painting is always a fun activity with not much preparation needed.*

Ginny Lyons:
"If you're going to make a craft in the classroom as one of your stations be sure to try it out at home to see how difficult and how long it takes."

Kim Davis:
"Its not fair that people who do the volunteering should always bring items needed. All parents should be used."

Beth Bear:
"When buying favors make sure it would appeal to both boys and girls."

17

Halloween School Parties:

Do you have any tips for room parents?

Debby Baldwin:
"Always play games first and have treats later."

Gloria Schwiesow:
1. *The basic thing for me is to keep it simple. A pizza party is easy if you have the money. Ice Cream sundaes are also easy.*

2. *Really know the kids and what they would like for their age.*

3. *Send out a letter with what is needed for the party. Have it donate.*

Paula Garb:
"As a working parent you can still participate in planning and assisting with room parenting. There are a lot of things that you can do at home in preparation for planning for your childs party."

Sandy Boyd:
"Set up party favors on children's desk while they are out of the room."

12. Parents should wear costumes if possible, because children like to see us dressed up. Dressing to fit the theme of the party helps to reinforce the theme. So the mom in charge of the pumpkin game could dress like a pumpkin. If the child is in the pumpkin group, he will know to start his rotation at the pumpkin mom's area.

13. Purchase or make extra favors because some may break and you may need others for new students who have joined the class.

14. Make sure you have an updated class list.

15. Check with the teacher on correct spelling of names if you are personalizing anything.

16. Ask the teacher if younger siblings can come to the parties. If the teacher says yes, ask your room parents to include extra treats, drinks, and favors, if possible. Always include drinks and treats for the teachers and parent helpers. Favors for the teachers would also be nice. They can give them to their children or save them to give to students who lose theirs.

17. Many room parents may have more than one child attending the school. They need to be aware that it is very difficult for other room helpers if they party hop. This problem can be solved by going to Chris's Halloween party and Amy's Valentine's Day party. If a mother has more than two children at the school, maybe the father can help by working in one of the other children's classes.

18. Try to keep all the plans a secret from your child who will attend the party. He/she will enjoy the party more that way.

19. Downplay the scary aspect of Halloween for younger children. Go for cute, fun, and silly.

20. Have everything ready before the party begins.

21. Don't forget your camera, film, and/or video recorder.

22. Keep in contact with the teacher about all party plans including food.

23. For more hints, read all the helpful hints which you will find before each chapter.

24. Finally, start and end on time.

25. Have fun!

Party Report Form

Party Date & Time: _____

Teacher/Grade: _____

Head Room Parent: _____

Budget: _____

How much was spent?:_____

How much was left?: _____

Refreshments served: _____

    Treats: 1._____   Drinks: 1._____

           2._____   2._____

Games and/or Craft Activities:_____
(briefly describe each and use back if necessary, include prizes if any.)

    1. _____

    2. _____

    3. _____

    4. _____

    5. _____

    6. _____

Take Home Favors: _____

    1. _____

    2. _____

    3. _____

    4. _____

    5. _____

    6. _____

What Worked: _____

_____

What Didn't Work:_____

_____

How Many Parents Attended the Party?: _____

Please return to the Room Parent Coordinator or PTO box within one week
of the party. Thank you!

NOTES:_____

_____

_____

_____

_____

_____

_____

_____

_____

_____

_____

_____

_____

_____

_____

_____

_____

_____

_____

_____

_____

_____

_____

_____

_____

_____

19

Room Parents Assignment List

NOTES:_____

_____

_____

_____

_____

_____

_____

_____

_____

_____

_____

_____

_____

_____

_____

_____

_____

_____

_____

_____

_____

_____

_____

Party Date & Time:_____

Teacher/Grade:_____

Head Room Parent:_____

Budget:_____

Teacher Suggestions:_____

Room Parent Helpers:_____

_____

Clean-up:_____ Set-up:_____

Nametags:_____

Treats: 1._____   Drinks: 1._____

2._____   2._____

Plasticware:_____   Punch Bowl:_____

Napkins:_____   Cups:_____

Plates:_____   Ice:_____

Games and/or Craft Activities: _____   Prizes:_____

1._____

2._____

3._____

4._____

5._____

6._____

Take Home Favors:_____

1._____

2._____

3._____

4._____

5._____

6._____

Favor Bags:_____

_____

_____

20

NOTES

CHAPTER TWO
Games

Helpful Hints for Games

1. Read the introduction for important game information.

2. Give all the children a chance to play. Some children do not want to participate, but let them choose.

3. Keep games short: five minutes long for younger students (grades K-2) and ten minutes for older ones (grades 3-6).

4. Keep all directions simple, because kids are tired of listening all day long. Party time is party time.

5. Be flexible, if a game is not working well, stop playing it and start a different game.

6. Have a game (two would be great) in reserve in case one is not working well, or the games you planned went faster than you thought they would. A perfect example: Hidden Halloween words.

7. It is best not to play "elimination" games unless you have something for the children that are eliminated to do. If you have nothing planned, this leads to excess noise, running around, and chaos. In this situation, all you need is a simple activity such as guessing how many candy corns are in a jar.

8. Masking tape placed on the floor works well for a starting line. Move it closer for younger grades and farther back for older grades.

9. Remember to keep all games, prizes, etc. safe for children.

10. If you have more than one game going on at the same time have all games equal in time. This will allow all stations to rotate at the same time.

11. Try to have one parent at each game station. Some games where you retrieve balls, bean bags etc. goes smoother and faster if there are two helping parents.

12. If you are using rotating stations have one person tell the class when to rotate. They can do this with turning the class lights on and off.

13. While games are being played have a parent get refreshments ready, if you are eating after the games are over.

14. Items used to play games can also be used as their take home favors. Examples, bean bags (Beat the Bat), ping pong balls (Frankenstein's Eyeballs).

15. If you have finished your game and are not ready to rotate to another game, you may read some of the Knowledge Facts, or let the kids play the game again.

Bat Games

Flying Bats (K-2)

Supplies

Child-size fishing pole
  or
Wooden dowel and heavy string
Magnet
Black construction paper
Paper clips
Container (small wading pool or large
  box) for bat cut-outs

Directions

1. Attach a magnet to the end of a child-size fishing pole or attach a string near the end of a wooden dowel, securing a magnet to the opposite end of the string.

2. Cut bat shapes out of black construction paper. Glue paper clips on the mouth area of the bats.

3. Place several cut-out bats into a container such as a child's wading pool or a box painted black. Decorate the container with round white moons. Add black cut-out bats over the moons.

4. Children fish and try to catch bats inside the container. When the magnet "hooks" onto the bat, the student can pull out the pole and watch the bat fly!

Bats in a Cave (K-6)

Supplies

Small plastic bat
  (to fit in palm of hand)
Variation: Three small plastic bats

Bats are the only mammals that can fly. They find their way around in the dark by listening with their ears to sounds and their echoes. The old saying " You're as blind as a bat!" is not true. Although bats don't have good eyesight, they aren't blind. But if they were they could still find their way around in the dark by listening.

Directions

1. Have the class sit in a circle on the floor.

2. Turn off the lights and have the kids pass a plastic bat around the circle, each child passing the bat quickly to the child next to them.

3. When you turn on the light whoever has the bat is eliminated.

4. Continue to play for a set amount of time or until all players are eliminated.

5. To make this game more challenging for older grades, use two or three bats going around the circle in opposite directions.

Beat the Bat (K-6)

Supplies

Bat Halloween fabric
Beans (uncooked)
Five coffee cans with lids,
   same size
White construction paper
Black construction paper
Masking tape

Directions

1. Sew three bean bags using Halloween fabric. Material with bats on it would look great.

2. Remove the plastic lids. Cover the cans with white construction paper. Replace the plastic lids.

3. Decorate the cans with white round moons and black bats made from construction paper.

4. Stack the cans on a child's desk. Line up three cans on the bottom row, then two on top of them, and one more on top of those two to form a pyramid.

5. Use masking tape to make a line on the ground which the children must stand behind when throwing the bean bags at the cans. Place the line farther back for older kids.

6. Give each child three tries to throw the bean bags in order to try to knock all the cans off the desk. This game is noisy but popular with kids of all ages.

7. Restack the cans for the next child's turn.

   Note: This game will rotate faster if two helpers can retrieve cans and stack them.

Bat Coin Toss (K-6)

Supplies

Black construction paper
Goblets
Six Pennies
Masking tape
Cooking oil
Napkins

Directions

1. Cut bat shapes out of black construction paper.

2. Tape the bats onto clear goblets or glasses and line them up on a desk in the shape of a bat. Give the children six pennies a piece.

3. Determine a starting line and mark it with masking tape.

4. The object is to toss the pennies into the goblets and have them stay. If you want to make the game harder for older kids, move the starting line back. Another way to make the game more difficult is to wipe the glasses with a napkin that has cooking oil on it. The oil makes the glasses slippery so that it is harder for the pennies to stay in them.

Bat Volleyball (K-6)

Supplies

Black balloons
White glow-in-the-dark paint

Directions

1. Before the party, blow up the balloons and decorate them with bat faces.

2. For younger grades (K-1), have the kids sit on their chairs in a small circle. Tell them that they must stay seated during the entire game. Hit the balloon into the air, then let the kids keep hitting it up until it touches the floor, and a new round begins.

3. For older kids (2-6 grade), divide the kids in half. You now have team A and team B. Have the kids sit on their chairs in two rows facing each other. Tell them to hit the balloon back and forth similar to volleyball. For a harder game, play in the dark with a balloon painted with glow-in-the-dark paints.

4. Keep score for the older kids only. When one team (team A) hits the ball and it falls (on the ground) on the opposite teams' side (team B) they (team A) score a point. A total of 15 points wins the game. Remember: Children must stay seated at all times.

A cave is a popular place for bats to hibernate. But a bat doesn't need to hibernate if it lives where it will stay warm all year long. A bat that does hibernate in a cave likes to be up high in crevices.

27

Bat! Bat! Who Has the Bat? (K-2)

Supplies
One to three tiny plastic bats (small enough to fit in palm of hand)

What makes a school Halloween party fun?

David Krohn, 7 years old:
"Moms helping you."

Nick Ripple, 10 years old:
"The games."

Pamela Kortman, 9 years old:
"All of the games and spending time with other moms."

Directions

1. This is played like "Button! Button! Who has the Button?", except you use a tiny plastic bat.

2. Choose a child to hold the bat. He will be called the starter.

3. The other kids sit in a circle with their hands held out with palms touching. The starter stands in the middle of the circle.

4. The starter holds the bat inside of his hands held the same way as the other kids.

5. He goes around the inside of the circle pretending to drop the bat into each child's hands.

6. He does drop it into a classmates' hands but continues to play for a few more minutes so no one knows where he left the bat.

7. He stops and stands in the middle and repeats the chant: "Bat! Bat! Who has the bat?"

8. Whoever guesses what child has the bat goes to the middle of the circle to be the starter.

9. Repeat the game.

Supplies for Bat Games

Flying Bats (K-2)

Child-size fishing pole
  or
Wooden dowel and heavy string
Magnet
Black construction paper
Paper clips
Container (small wading pool or
  large box) for bat cut-outs

Bats in a Cave (K-6)

Small plastic bat (to fit in palm
  of hand)
Variation: Three small plastic bats

Beat the Bat (K-6)

Bat Halloween fabric
Beans (uncooked)
Five coffee cans with lids,
  same size
White construction paper
Black construction paper
Masking tape

Bat Coin Toss (K-6)

Black construction paper
Goblets
Six Pennies
Masking tape
Cooking oil
Napkins

Bat Volleyball (K-6)

Black balloons
White glow-in-the-dark paint

Bat! Bat! Who Has the Bat? (K-2)

One to three tiny plastic bats
  (small enough to fit in palm
  of hand)

Don't forget the camera and film.

Cat Games

Silly Cat Tricks (K-6)

Supplies

1" x ½" plain note paper (one per student)
Paper hole punch
Black yarn
Treats

Directions

1. Create a list of silly tricks for kids to perform. Write each trick on a separate piece of paper. You'll need one per student. Examples of tricks: 1. Do a cartwheel. 2. Sing. 3. Say the ABCs backwards. 4. Do ten sit-ups. 5. Write your name on the chalkboard backwards.

2. With a hole puncher, punch holes in the papers, slide yarn through the holes and secure each paper in series by tying a knot in the yarn. Leave about two feet between each paper.

3. After all the papers are on the yarn, wrap the yarn up into a big ball so no tricks show.

4. Have the children form a circle. Starting with any player, have them unwrap the yarn one by one until they reach a trick. The child pulls off that trick.

5. Have them perform the trick for a treat. No trick, no treat!

6. Continue until all players have had a turn.

   Note: Treats can be candy, stickers, and small trinkets. Be creative; make the treat something they want or they might not want to do the trick. For older grades, cans of pop and bags of candy or chips work well. Wrapping the treats will keep up the suspense throughout the game. Let the kids unwrap their treats after everyone has played.

Wild Cat Toss (K-6)

Supplies

Three stuffed animal cats
Three tennis balls
Brown construction paper (optional)

Directions

1. Line up stuffed animal cats on a child's desk, making believe the desk is a fence. If you'd like, decorate the desk to look like a fence using construction paper.

2. The object is to try to knock down the cats by throwing balls at them. Each child gets three shots. Mark the starting line with masking tape.

3. Position this game so that the balls are being tossed in the direction of an empty wall.

There is a type of cat called a wildcat. It lives in the mountains. Wildcats are strong and can be extremely cruel. During the day they sleep. At night, they go out to find food. This type of cat, like most, loves fish.

Frightened Cats (K-6)

Supplies

Polaroid film (one snapshot per student)
Polaroid camera
3" x 1" sticky labels
Permanent markers

Directions

1. Push two desks together. One by one, have each child lie back on the desks with his or her head hanging over the edge.

2. Comb through their hair with your fingers — or ask another child to do this — to make the hair wild and scary looking.

3. Kneel so you are level with their face. Ask the wild cat (child) to look frightened, then take a photo.

4. Turn the picture so the child's face is right side up. On a sticky label, write the child's name with a permanent marker and fill in a reason why the student might be frightened. Ask the children for suggestions. (For example: "Jennifer frightened by a ghoul friend.")

5. Attach the sticky note to the bottom of the picture. This is a popular favor.

Jennifer frightened by:
_ _ _ _ _ _

Meow Meow (K-6)

Supplies

Cardboard box or wood board
Three embroidery hoops
Five cat related items, such as
    1. Cat food
    2. Toy mouse
    3. Box of cat litter
    4. Cat treats
    5. Stuffed animal cat
Masking tape

Directions

1. On a piece of wood, glue or tape down five cat-related items. The embroidery hoops should be large enough to fit over each item, because this is a ring-toss game.

2. Mark the starting line with masking tape.

3. Give each child three tries to ring the items. A ring must fall completely over an item to count. Give a point value to each item if you would like to make this game competitive. Older grades are more competitive and like to know their scores.

31

Cat Eyes (K-2)

Supplies

Poster board
Markers or paints
Blindfold
Round, colored self-adhesive labels (two
    per student)
Masking tape

If a male cat wanders into another cat's territory, the cat who lives there will fight with the intruder. A cat will try to protect it's territory by spraying urine or rubbing parts of its body on trees and shrubs.

Directions

1. On the poster board, draw black cats sitting on top of a fence. Add some color to the drawing if you'd like.

2. Place the poster board level with the children's heights, possibly on the chalkboard ledge or taped on a door or wall.

3. Determine your starting line and mark it with masking tape.

When a cat is frightened, it lowers its tail, arches its back, and all its hair stands up.

4. Play this game like "Pin the Tail on the Donkey." Hand the kids some cat eyes, then blindfold them one at a time, turning them around three times before directing them towards the drawing. The object is to get the cats' eyes into the correct area.

5. Use round colored self-adhesive labels for the eyes. If you mark the children's names on the labels you will be able to show them who won by getting closest to the correct area.

Clever Cat Quiz (3-6)

Supplies
Paper and Pencil

Directions

1. Give each child a piece of lined paper and a pencil.

2. Have them number lines from 1 to 16.

3. Ask them the questions listed below, explaining that all the answers start with the word cat. Before beginning, give them an example such as "What cat is a child's string game?" Answer: Cat's Cradle.

What cat causes a sudden disaster ?
Catastrophe

What cat breeds cattle?
Cattleman

What cat is a narrow walkway?
Catwalk

What cat is a tall reed like marsh plant?
Cattail

What cat sleeps lightly?
Cat Nap

What cat is a member of a church?
Catholic

What cat is a girls name?
Catherine

What cat likes to be in water?
Catfish

What cat will turn into a butterfly or moth?
Caterpillar

What cat likes to hang out in a group?
Category

What cat likes to play baseball?
*Catch*er

What cat breaks into houses?
Cat Burglar

What cat roams in an underground cemetery with tunnels?
Catacomb

What cat floats on water?
Catamaran

What cat is sent in the mail?
Catalogue

What cat lives on a range in New York state?
Catskill Mountains

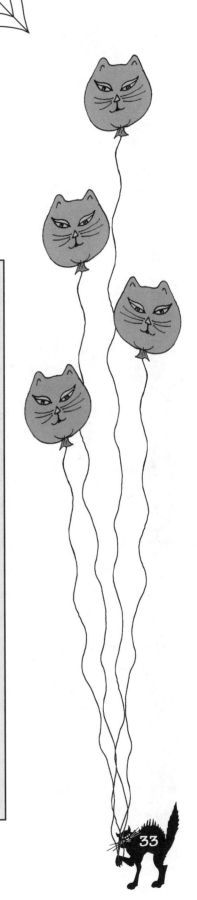

33

Supplies for Cat Games

Silly Cat Tricks (K-6)

1" x 1/2" plain note paper (one per
 student)
Paper hole punch
Black yarn
Treats

Wild Cat Toss (K-6)

Three stuffed animal cats
Three tennis balls
Brown construction paper
 (optional)

Frightened Cats (K-6)

Polaroid Film (one snapshot per
 student)
Polaroid Camera
3" x 1" Sticky labels
Permanent Markers

Meow Meow (K-6)

Cardboard box or wood board
Three embroidery hoops

Five cat related items, such as
 1. Cat food
 2. Toy mouse
 3. Box of cat litter
 4. Cat treats
 5. Stuffed animal cat
Masking tape

Cat Eyes (K-2)

Poster board
Markers or paints
Blindfold
Round, colored self-adhesive labels
 (two per student)
Masking tape

Clever Cat Quiz (3-6)

Paper and Pencil

Don't forget the camera and film.

Frankenstein Games

Frankenstein's Makeup (3-6)

Supplies

Towels or wet wipes
Any of the following ingredients:
  peanut butter
  cake frosting
  mayonnaise
  ketchup
  cream cheese
  toothpaste
  cool whip
  shaving cream
  jelly
  sour cream
Bowls
Spoons
Awards

For a green face try one of the following:

Version #1	Version #2	For a Red Scar
Unflavored gelatin Water Green food coloring	2 teaspoons of cornstarch 1 teaspoon of water 1 teaspoon cold cream Green food coloring	Corn syrup Cold cream Red food coloring

Mary Shelley was only 19 years old when she wrote her classic thriller, *Frankenstein*, in 1818.

Directions

1. Form teams of one girl and one boy each.

2. The girls use the ingredients (listed above) on the boys faces to create a Frankenstein-look.

3. The boys sit in chairs at their desks and the girls stand.

4. All the "makeup" that a girl needs should be placed on her partner's desk.

5. Allow five minutes for face painting. Have the teacher and helpers judge winners in the following categories:

   Cleanest   Unusual overall design
   Creative use of ingredients   Best attitudes.

6. The judges start judging each team as it finishes. This way there is not a big wait for cleanup.

7. Have the boys use wet towels or wet wipes to get clean. If you are lucky enough to have a sink in the room, have the boys wash with water and soap and dry with towels.

8. Have the girls clean up the desks while the boys clean their faces.

9. Give awards.

Frankenstein's Laboratory (3-6)

Supplies

Cooked spaghetti or wet sponge
Peeled grapes or green olives
Chicken bones
Rubber glove
Cooked rice
Dried apricots
Gelatin dessert (prepared as per
  directions)
Small dried carrots
Dried beans
Cocktail franks
French cut string beans
Ten small boxes
Poster board
Optional: A helper dressed like
  Frankenstein

In 1910, Universal Pictures made a silent film based on Mary Wollstonecraft Shelley's novel *Frankenstein*. It was produced by Thomas Alva Edison. In 1931, Boris Karloff played the monster in the original talking version of the movie. In 1935, there was a sequel titled *Bride of Frankenstein*, which also starred Boris Karloff. Karloff then appeared in the 1939 movie *Son of Frankenstein*. Movies about the famous monster continued to be made with *Ghost of Frankenstein* in 1942, *Frankenstein Meets the Wolf Man* in 1943, and *House of Frankenstein* in 1944. The movie *Abbott and Costello Meet Frankenstein* came out in 1948 and was followed by *Curse of Frankenstein* (1957) and *I was a Teenage Frankenstein* (1957). Do you remember *The Munsters*, a T.V. show that previewed in 1964? The father, Herman Munster, was made up to look like the Frankenstein monster. Finally, in 1974, there was a T.V. special *Frankenstein, The True Story*. That year, director Mel Brooks made the hilarious movie *Young Frankenstein*.

What makes a school Halloween party fun?

Timothy Laurie, 6 years old:
"Frankenstein's laboratory."

Directions

1. Make some signs saying "Please do not touch."

2. Place the items listed above in sealed boxes, each of which has a cut-out slot into which children can slide a hand to feel the items.

3. Label the boxes as suggested below but *do not* list the actual ingredient on the label.

   - Brains - Spaghetti
   - Eyeballs - peeled grapes or green olives
   - Bones - chicken bones
   - Hand - Rubber glove filled with frozen water or cooked rice.
   - Ears - Dried apricots
   - Guts - Gelatin dessert
   - Toes - Small dried up carrots
   - Teeth - beans
   - Fingers - Cocktail, franks
   - Veins - French cut string beans

4. Be even more creative by turning a section of the classroom into a "laboratory" with lots of signs and a parent dressed like Frankenstein, who greets the students at the entrance and helps them tour the laboratory.

Frankenstein's Eyeballs (K-6)

Supplies

Ping pong balls (one per child)
Permanent markers
Two spoons

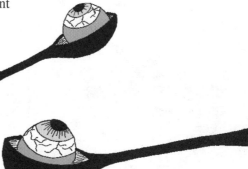

Directions

1. Previous to the party, paint eyeballs on ping pong balls with permanent markers.

2. Form two teams and divide each team into two.

3. Have half of one team stand on one side of the room and the other half stand on the opposite side of the room.

4. Do the same for the second team.

5. Give the first child in each line on one side of the room a spoon and place an "eyeball" in it.

6. They must walk to the opposite side of the room and give the spoons to their teammates. They may not hold the eyeball with fingers or thumb. Then they stay on that side and move to the back of their team's line.

7. The teammate who is now holding the spoon proceeds to the opposite side, gives the spoon to another teammate, then moves to the end of that line. And so it goes, back and forth, until everyone has a turn.

8. If the eye falls off the spoon, the child retrieves it and returns to the starting line on the side of the room where the child received the spoon. The first team to finish is the winner.

9. The kids enjoy having an eyeball to take home as a favor. So look for gum ball eyes, eyeball ping pong balls, and eyeball rubber balls when out shopping if you would rather buy them than make your own.

Frank(en-steins) (K-6)

Supplies

Franks (hot dogs)
Steins (beer mugs or paper cups)
Four plastic spoons (and 2 spares)

Directions

1. Cut up franks (hot dogs) into pieces and have the kids toss them into (beer) steins placed beyond the starting line.

2. Mark your line with masking tape setting the line further back for older grades.

   Variation: For older grades place a piece of a hot dog on a plastic spoon and let the kids flip the tip of the spoon so the hot dog flies into the stein. Older kids love playing the game this way.

Frankenstein's Teeth (K-6)

Supplies

Two spatulas
Dried beans
Two bowls

Directions

1. Form two teams, then determine starting and finish lines.

2. Place an empty bowl at the finish line for each team.

3. At the starting line, have a bowl full of beans (teeth) and a spatula for each team.

4. The first player on each team picks up the spatula and scoops as many beans as possible from the team's bowl.

5. The player walks quickly to the finish line and dumps the beans into the bowl. Whatever beans drop, stay on the floor.

6. The player runs back to his team and hands the spatula to the next player in line to perform the same task.

7. When the time allotted is over, count the beans in each team's bowl at the finish line to determine who has the most and is the winner. Each team member might take two or possibly three turns depending on time.

   Optional: To increase the intensity, have the children spin in circles as they walk down to the finish line. They will have to concentrate or more beans will fall off their spatulas.

Frankenstein Says (K-6)

Supplies

No materials required

Directions

1. Play this game like "Simon Says," making sure to give the older children more difficult commands.

2. One child is chosen to be Frankenstein. He stands a few feet in front of the other classmates (facing the classmates).

3. Frankenstein gives a command such as "Frankenstein says do jumping jacks". If Frankenstein just gives the command "do jumping jacks" without saying "Frankenstein says" any players who do the jumping jacks are eliminated.

4. When all players are eliminated the game is over. Depending on your time frame, let other players take turns being Frankenstein.

5. It is best to play this in larger spaces than classrooms—possibly in the gym or cafeteria, or outside on the playground.

Supplies for Frankenstein Games

Frankenstein's Makeup (3-6)

Towels or wet wipes
Any of the following ingredients:

peanut butter	cake frosting
mayonnaise	ketchup
cream cheese	toothpaste
cool whip	shaving cream
jelly	sour cream

Bowls
Spoons
Awards
For a green face try one of
   the following:
Version #1.
     Unflavored gelatin
     Water
     Green food coloring.
Version #2
     2 teaspoons of cornstarch
     1 teaspoon of water
     1 teaspoon cold cream
     Green food coloring
Red Scar:
     Corn syrup
     Cold cream
     Red food coloring

Frankenstein's Laboratory (3-6)

Cooked spaghetti or wet sponge
Peeled grapes or green olives
Chicken bones
Rubber glove
Cooked rice
Dried apricots
Gelatin dessert (prepared as
   perdirections)

Small dried carrots
Dried beans
Cocktail franks
French cut string beans
Ten small boxes
Poster board
Optional: A helper dressed like
   Frankenstein

Frankenstein's Eyeballs (K-6)

Ping pong balls (one per child)
Permanent markers
Two spoons

Frank(en-steins) (K-6)

Franks (hot dogs)
Steins (beer mugs or paper cups)
Four plastic spoons (and 2 spares)

Frankenstein's Teeth (K-6)

Two spatulas
Dried beans
Two bowls

Frankenstein Says (K-6)

No materials required

Don't forget the camera and film.

Ghost Games

Ghosts in the Air (K-2)

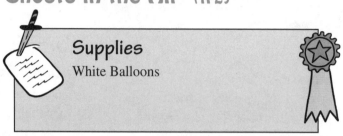

Supplies
White Balloons

Directions

1. Parent helpers blow up white balloons and, without tying the ends, release them into the air.

2. The children try to catch the balloons (ghosts) before they deflate and fall to the ground.

3. Due to concerns about not wanting to spread illness, don't let the children keep the balloons they catch. They might be tempted to blow them up again. Have the children turn the balloons in for a favor.

4. Stretching the balloons before you blow them up will make it easier. You need a lot of helpers blowing up balloons so that no one gets tired. (A small tank of helium would work great.)

Floating Ghosts (K-6)

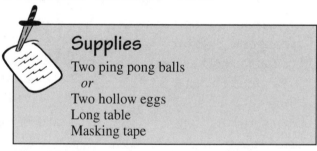

Supplies
Two ping pong balls
   or
Two hollow eggs
Long table
Masking tape

Directions:

1. Divide the class into two teams. Tell the children to hold their hands behind their backs. Station the teams at a long table opposite each other.

2. Mark goal lines with masking tape on each teams side.

3. Place a ping pong ball in the center of the long table.

4. The kids blow at the ball trying to get it to cross over into the other teams' goal area. If a ball falls off the table before entering the goal, place the ball in the center of the table again.

5. Keep score: One point for each goal made. Play for an allotted time or to 21 points. Variation: try an empty egg instead of a ping pong ball. Using a needle, pierce a hole at both ends of the egg, then blow the yolk and egg white out . Let the egg dry overnight. An egg adds a little twist, because it doesn't roll evenly. It is more challenging and fun. If you have a large group of kids on each side you may use two eggs or ping pong balls for more of a challenge.

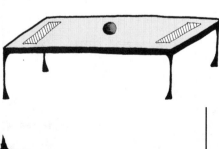

Ghost Faces (K-2)

Supplies

Powdered sugar
Candy
Individual paper plates

Directions

1. Sprinkle powdered sugar onto individual paper plates.
2. Hide a piece of candy under the sugar.
3. The children try to find the candy with their mouths (no hands allowed.)
4. They will look like little ghosts by the time they find the candy. Have your cameras ready.

   Note: Children with allergies or breathing problems probably should not participate in this game. As always, please check with the teacher or parents.

Haunting Ghosts (K-6)

Supplies

Cardboard box (approximately 18" x 24")
Paints
One sheet of white tissue paper
Two moving eyes
   or
Black marker
   or
Black felt
7" piece of yarn
Masking tape
A magazine

Directions

1. Decorate a cardboard box to look like a haunted house.
2. Cut out a doorway big enough to have the following ghost go through.
3. Tear a sheet of tissue paper in half, crumble up one half to form a ball. Form the other half around the ball to form the ghost's body. If necessary trim any excess paper off the body.
4. Tie a piece of yarn around the neck and fluff out the body.
5. Make two eyes with a black marker or glue on black felt or moving eyes.
6. Mark a starting line with masking tape. Put the ghost on the floor at the starting line.
7. Have the kids use a magazine to fan the ghosts through the door and into the haunted house.

A "ghostwriter" is someone who you hire to write anonymously for you (the employer). You pick a subject, the ghostwriter does the writing, and you are published as the author. Sometimes a ghostwriter uses the notes given to him or he does the research needed. You need a written agreement with the ghostwriter saying that you will be credited as the author, otherwise the ghostwriter can claim the copyright.

41

Use candy corn for markers

Ghost Bingo (K-6)

Supplies

Halloween candy
Paper to make bingo cards
Bingo calling numbers

Directions

1. Ghost bingo is played using Halloween candy such as candy corn for markers. Instruct the kids not to eat the candy during the game. Once the game is over they can.

2. For younger grades play regular bingo.

3. Rules for regular bingo: The caller draws out a number and the children mark that number if it is on their card. The first child who has all the numbers in one consecutive row wins. He then calls out "GHOST".

4. Play speedball bingo with the older grades.

5. Rules for speedball: The object is to cover each space on the bingo card (blackout). Announce the number twice very quickly. Do not repeat or display any numbers, the players must rely on good listening. The first player to reach a confirmed blackout wins. Speedball bingo is a challenge for all ages.

   Note: In speedball you may have to call out up to 60 numbers before someone wins.

6. When playing either bingo game, remember to have the kids call out "Ghost", not "Bingo", to win.

7. Use the following examples for your Ghost Bingo cards. Simply make copies for the class or copy onto treat bags.

"Bingo" oops I mean "Ghost" I win!

G	H	O	S	T
1-15	16-30	31-45	46-60	61-75
1	17	31	50	61
4	20	36	53	65
7	24	40	48	72
11	26	45	56	75
6	28	39	49	70

43

G 1-15	H 16-30	O 31-45	S 46-60	T 61-75
15	29	35	59	68
6	22	39	57	74
14	16	41	47	67
9	18	43	48	70
13	19	32	51	71

44

G	H	O	S	T
1-15	16-30	31-45	46-60	61-75
3	16	34	60	62
8	30	44	58	75
9	22	45	46	73
15	21	37	55	66
2	18	40	49	69

45

Halloween School Parties:

G 1-15	H 16-30	O 31-45	S 46-60	T 61-75
5	23	38	52	63
10	25	33	54	71
12	30	42	46	64
1	27	40	60	74
7	29	34	59	65

46

Ghost Story (K-6)

Supplies

Optional: Tape player and a blank tape

Directions

1. Seat the kids on the floor in a circle.

2. Have a parent start a ghost story and, going around the circle, ask each child to add a sentence to the story.

3. Meanwhile, another parent writes down or records the story so the children can listen to it during their snack time.

4. For a great favor, give each child a copy of the tape.

5. For younger grades, start a friendly story with a sentence such as "The friendly ghost went to the beach." For older grades you might start the story with "The ghosts were floating around in the graveyard."

Marshmallow Ghosts (K-6)

Supplies

Marshmallows
Thread
Black decorating gel
Broom

Directions

1. Tie each marshmallow with a long piece of thread.

2. Dot with two eyes.

3. Tie the thread to the broomstick. For older kids, have a parent helper hold the broomstick up high and wave it a bit to make the ghosts "fly." For younger kids, the helper should hold the broomstick still.

4. Without using their hands, the kids try to capture the floating ghost with their mouths.

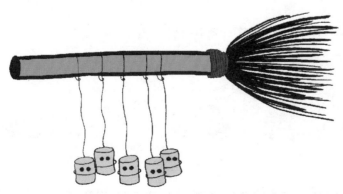

Do ghosts really exist? Here is an explanation of why ghosts supposedly walk through walls: Ghosts use a path that they were used to when they were alive. But, if a house has gone through remodeling and some of the structure has changed (for example, there is a wall where there once was a door), ghosts will walk right through the walls like they used to when they were alive. This also explains why they might climb stairs that no longer exist.

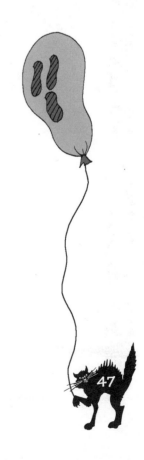

47

Supplies for Ghost Games

Ghosts in the Air (K-2)

White Balloons

Floating Ghosts (K-6)

Two ping pong balls
   or
Two hollow eggs
Long table
Masking tape

Ghost Faces (K-2)

Powdered sugar
Candy
Individual paper plates

Haunting Ghosts (K-6)

Cardboard box
   (approximately 18" x 24")
Paints
One sheet of white tissue paper
Two moving eyes
   or

Black marker
   or
Black felt
7" piece of yarn
Masking tape
A magazine

Ghost Bingo (K-6)

Halloween candy
Paper to make bingo cards
Bingo calling numbers

Ghost Story (K-6)

Optional: Tape player and a blank
   tape

Marshmallow Ghosts (K-6)

Marshmallows
Thread
Black decorating gel
Broom

Don't forget the camera and film.

Pumpkin Games

Pumpkin Bean Bag Toss (K-6)

Supplies

36" x 48" plywood
40" x 52" orange felt
20" x 6" orange felt
20" x 6" black felt
Tacky glue
Thread and needle
Beans (uncooked)
Masking tape

Directions

1. In the weeks before the party, cut a pumpkin shape out of a large piece of plywood. Give it some character by cutting a mouth, nose, and two eyes. Cover the plywood with orange felt. (Tacky glue works well with felt.)

2. Sew six pumpkin shaped bean bags using the following pattern. Sew three orange pumpkins (with black faces) and three black pumpkins (with orange faces).

3. Use the facial patterns for the pumpkins eyes, nose, and mouth. Sew or attach with tacky glue.

4. Use a zig zag stitch to sew the two pieces of orange felt together (right sides facing out) leaving an opening to stuff in the beans. The zig zag stitch will give the bean bag a decorative look and makes it easier than turning the bag inside out.

5. Designate your starting line with masking tape on the floor.

6. Determine how many tosses you will allow per child.

7. Move your line closer for the younger children, farther back for older ones.

8. The object is to get the bean bags through the plywood pumpkin's mouth, nose, or eyes. Surprisingly, this is an all-time favorite of all ages.

What makes a school Halloween party fun?

Derek O'Neil, 11 years old:
"Pumpkin bean bag toss and candy."

Timothy Laurie, 6 years old:
Pumpkin bean bag toss."

Allison Knight, 6 years old:
"Making jack-o-lanterns."

Drenched Pumpkins (K-6)

Supplies

Two carved pumpkins
Four water spray bottles
Four to six votive candles
Matches
Plastic backdrop
Masking tape

What makes a school Halloween party fun?

Kali O'Neil, 8 years old:
"Making a bunch of decorations."

Christie Day, 10 years old:
"The costumes."

Directions

This game is ideal for outdoor play. Since it involves lit candles and spray bottles, be sure to check with your school to see if these items may be used indoors or outside. A parent must always be at this station.

1. Purchase two pumpkins of the same size.

2. Carve out jack-o-lantern style, giving each a big mouth.

3. Place a votive candle inside each pumpkin.

4. Mark your starting line with masking tape.

5. Form two teams. Give each team a water-filled spray bottle.

6. Light the candles.

7. Depending on the power of the spray bottles, the children may need to be one to three feet away from the pumpkins. The kids take turns squirting water into the pumpkin's mouth trying to extinguish the flame.

8. If played inside, use a backdrop behind and under the pumpkins to catch the water.

    Note: It is best to have one parent helper supervising the game while a second helper continuously reloads water into additional spray bottles. Also, it is best to have extra votive candles in case the wax on the originals gets too wet to re-light.

Silly Pumpkin Relay (K-6)

Supplies

Orange construction paper
Marker
Masking tape

Directions

1. Think of lots of different relay race activities (perhaps 12) the kids can do such as: Walk backwards, walk like a caterpillar, leap, skip, hop, do a cartwheel, jump like a bunny and do a somersault.

2. Make pumpkin shapes out of construction paper (one per student). Dividing the number of pumpkins in half, write a different activity on each pumpkin in the first group. Repeat this procedure with the second group so that you have two sets of the same activities.

3. Form two teams and mark your starting line with masking tape.

4. The pumpkin shapes are placed in two piles on the floor across the room with one pile opposite each team.

5. The first child on each team runs to that team's pile of pumpkin shapes, picks one up and performs the activity while heading back towards the child's team.

6. The next team member goes.

7. The first team to finish wins.

There are a lot of varieties of pumpkins to choose from. Connecticut Field and Howden are two popular brands. Call your state agriculture department to see if these pumpkins are grown locally. It makes for a fun day to go to the pumpkin farm.

Pumpkin Shootout (K-6)

Supplies

Plywood or orange poster board
Paints
Crossbow/foam shooting arrows
Masking tape

Directions

1. Before the party, draw five pumpkin shapes of different sizes on plywood or orange poster board. Cut them out. If you use plywood, paint it orange. (The wood version can be saved for many years of use.)

2. Give each pumpkin-shaped opening a point value.

3. Using masking tape, designate a line behind which participants stand when shooting.

4. Give each player three tries to shoot the objects into the cut out pumpkin holes.

5. Add the point values. The highest total wins.

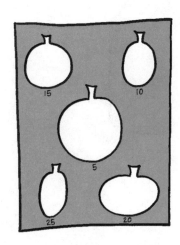

Pumpkin Hop (K-6)

Supplies

Orange construction paper (about 20 sheets)
Marker
Masking tape

Directions

1. This game can be played with one team or more.

2. Place six to ten large pumpkin cut-outs (made from construction paper) per team in a crooked line on the floor. It is best to tape these down so there will be no shifting.

3. Designate starting and finish lines with masking tape.

4. Have each team line up at its starting line. The children will hop from the first pumpkin to the last pumpkin in the order they were placed on the floor. If a child misses the pumpkin they go back to the starting line and starts over.

5. When a child reaches the finish line, the next team member may go and repeat the process.

6. The first team to finish wins.

7. For younger children, place the pumpkins closer together and have the kids hop on two feet.

8. For older children, place the pumpkins farther apart and have the kids hop on one foot.

9. It helps if the pumpkins are marked with consecutive numbers or alphabet letters. This way, the younger students can practice counting or reciting the alphabet. For older grades, spell the numbers in different languages or use math problems to direct them. An example of a math problem: "two times three plus four equal ten."

What makes a school Halloween party fun?

Rachel Laurie, 7 years old:
"The decorations."

Katie Day, 6 years old:
"The costumes."

Chelsea Alles, 8 years old:
"The costumes."

Pumpkin Toss (K-6)

Supplies

Six carved pumpkins (all the same size)
  or
Six plastic pumpkins (all the same size)
Three ping pong balls
Masking tape

Directions

1. Carve six pumpkins jack-o-lantern style with their lids removed. Or use plastic pumpkins. Place them directly behind one another in a line.

2. Determine a starting line marked with masking tape.

3. Mark the pumpkins one through six.

4. Give the player a ping pong ball to toss into the first pumpkin.

5. If they player succeeds provide a prize and have the player continue on to pumpkin number two, and so forth. Give a prize each time the ball makes it into the next numbered pumpkin. If the player misses a pumpkin, the player's turn is over and the next person tries.

6. This game can also be played for points by putting a number on each pumpkin—for example, 5,10,15, 20, 25, 30.

7. Prizes can be stickers, stamps on their hands, books, candy, trinkets, etc.

Variation: Scatter the pumpkins instead of placing them in a straight line. Let each child have three balls to toss. Add up the points at the end of a player's turn.

Many years ago, a material called "composition" (similar to Plaster of Paris) was used to make Jack-O-Lanterns. Tissue paper was combined with composition to form the facial features. Years later, pressed cardboard and paperboard came into use. In the 1930s, lightweight paper-mâché gained popularity. By the 1950s plastic was being used to make Jack-O-Lanterns. Battery-powered light bulbs began being substituted for a candle inside Jack-O-Lanterns.

Supplies for Pumpkin Games

Pumpkin Bean Bag Toss (K-6)

36" x 48" plywood
40" x 52" orange felt
20" x 6" orange felt
20" x 6" black felt
Tacky glue
Thread and needle
Beans (uncooked)
Masking tape

Drenched Pumpkins (K-6)

Two carved pumpkins
Four water spray bottles
Four to six votive candles
Matches
Plastic backdrop
Masking Tape

Silly Pumpkin Relay (K-6)

Orange construction paper
Marker
Masking tape

Pumpkin Shootout (K-6)

Plywood or orange poster board
Paints
Crossbow/foam shooting arrows
Masking tape

Pumpkin Hop (K-6)

Orange construction paper (about
    20 sheets)
Marker
Masking tape

Pumpkin Toss (K-6)

Six carved pumpkins (all the
    same size)
    or
Six plastic pumpkins (all the
    same size)
Three ping pong balls
Masking tape

Don't forget the camera and film.

Skeleton Games

Hang The Skeleton (K-6)

Directions

1. This is played like the spelling game "Hangman."

2. Make the bone pieces out of white poster board using the pattern on page 111.

3. Assign one child to do the writing and another to do the "hanging." The other kids can be thinkers.

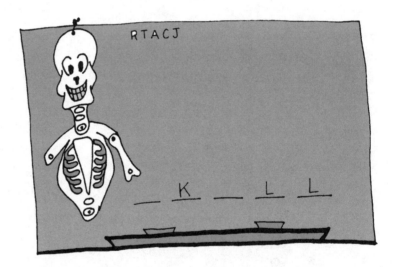

4. Before the party brainstorm a list of Halloween or spelling words that the children are likely to know. The teacher might be able to help you choose appropriate words.

5. Have the child who will do the writing choose a word. Depending on how many letters are in the word, mark that many blank spaces on the chalkboard. Decide how to rig the hanging skeleton near the chalkboard.

6. Have the kids take turns guessing letters. If the letter chosen is in the word, the writer fills in the correct blank. If not, the "hangman" places a skeleton bone using paper fasteners to attach it.

7. Start with the skeleton's head, proceed to the neck and shoulders, then the hips, arms, and leg pieces.

8. The kids have to guess the word before all the skeleton's bones are hung to win.

Animals that do not have a bony skeleton inside their body have what is called an exoskeleton, which is a hard external covering. An example is a beetle. However, a turtle has a hard exoskeleton on the outside of its body as well as a bony skeleton on ts inside.

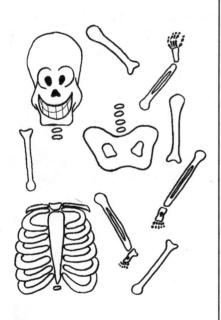

Pass The Skeleton (K-6)

Supplies
Chicken bones (one per team)
Ball of string per team (approximately three feet per player)

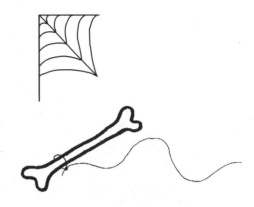

Directions

1. Form two or more teams. Give each team a chicken bone tied to a long string.

2. The first player pushes the bone up his sleeve, across his chest and down the other sleeve. He then passes the bone to the next teammate.

3. This procedure is repeated until the whole team is connected by the string.

4. The first team connected is the winner.

   Tip: The string can easily become tangled. Do not unwind the string from the ball until you're at school. Can you hear the giggles?

Cartilage (a firm, elastic, flexible type of connective tissue) is what makes up the skeleton of a dogfish. It has no bones.

Skeleton Bone Hunt (K-2)

Supplies
Chicken bones or dog bones
Small tub or wading pool
Styrofoam packing "peanuts" or sand

or Hide the pumpkins

Directions

1. If you use chicken bones, wash then boil them for five minutes to sterilize.

2. Hide several chicken bones in a small plastic wading pool or a tub filled with packing "peanuts" or sand.

3. Have small groups of children search for as many bones as they can find.

4. Collect all the bones and re-hide them for the next group of children.

   Variation: Paint a number on each bone and let the children retrieve only one bone each. The number on each bone will correspond to a prize.

   Note: Styrofoam packing "peanuts" cling and can make a mess. It is best to use a deep container that is filled only half way with the peanuts. This will help to keep the "peanuts" in the container.

Skeleton Straw Game (K-6)

Supplies

White copy paper
Straws (one per student)
Note: For chicken bones, ask at your
    local grocer for leftover bones.

Direction

1. Draw skeleton bones (one per child) on plain white copy paper. Cut them out.

2. Give a bone and a straw to each child.

3. The children take turns walking from one side of the room to the other while sucking in on the straw to create a vacuum that holds the paper bone in place.

4. You can make this a team game if you'd like.

Jumbled Shivering Bones (1-6)

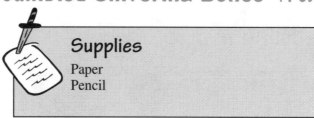

Supplies

Paper
Pencil

Directions:

1. This is a word jumble game. Give each child a copy of the bone word list below. Tell them that the column on the right represents bones that got all shook up and that they need to help put them back in order.

Children have 300 bones. Their bones will fuse together as they grow. An adult has 206 bones. The longest bone is the thigh (femur) bone. One of the three bones in the middle ear is the smallest bone.

Grades (3-6)		**Grades (1-2)**	
1. Femur (thigh bone)	eurmf	1. Leg	gle
2. Tibia (Shin bone)	biati	2. Hip	pih
3. Fibula (calf bone)	ubilaf	3. Tail	ailt
4. Coccyx (tail bone)	cyxocc	4. Funny	nunyf
5. Cranium (skull)	rimucan	5. Ankle	kanle
6. Zygoma (cheek bones)	amgoz	6. Shin	nhis
7. Phalanges (toe bones)	lapgeshan	7. Heel	eleh
8. Calcaneus (heel bone)	clanuesca	8. Rib	bri
9. Patella (knee cap)	atlaple	9. Foot	ooft
10. Metacarpal (hand bone)	earaalcmtp	10. Back	kacb
11. Humerus (upper arm bone)	rusumhe	11. Skull	kulsl
12. Clavicle (collar bone)	vlacicle	12. Collar	olracl

2. If you feel you need to make the game easier, give the answers to the jumbles on the bottom of the page. The kids can cross the correct names off as they decode the words.

Musical Bones (K-4)

Supplies
White poster board
Music

Directions

1. This game is played like musical chairs.

2. Draw several bone shapes on white poster board and cut them out.

3. Place the bones on a round table (refer to drawing). There should be one less bone than there are children.

4. The children walk around the table while music plays.

5. When the music stops the children all try to grab a bone.

6. The child who doesn't retrieve a bone is eliminated from the game.

7. Take away another bone and play another round.

8. There always needs to be one less bone than the number of players.

9. Have each child who is eliminated take a turn starting and stopping the music.

Did you know that in the morning you are taller than when you go to bed at night. Try this test: Back up to a wall and have a parent mark your height. To get an accurate measurement lay a book flat on top of your head. Do this at night, then in the morning. The reason this happens is that, while you are sleeping, water swells up in the disks which is between the vertebra of your spine. During the day, gravity and movement squeezes the water out.

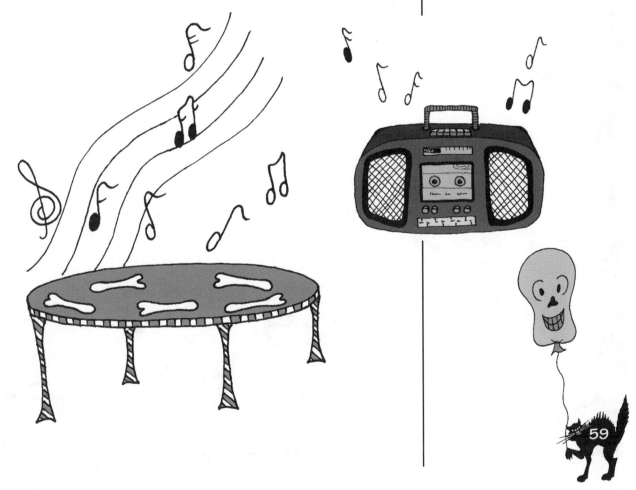

Supplies for Skeleton Games

Hang The Skeleton (K-6)

White poster board
Paper fasteners
Paper puncher

Pass The Skeleton (K-6)

Chicken bones (one per team)
Ball of string per team (approximatly three feet per player)

Skeleton Bone Hunt (K-2)

Chicken bones or dog bones
Small tub or wading pool
Styrofoam packing "peanuts"
   or sand

Skeleton Straw Game (K-6)

White copy paper
Straws (one per student)
Note For chicken bones, ask at your
   local grocer for leftover bones.

Jumbled Shivering Bones (1-6)

Paper
Pencil

Musical Bones (K-4)

White poster board
Music

Don't forget the camera and film.

Spider Games

Spider Cube Melt (K-6)

Supplies
Ice cube trays or paper cups
Small plastic spiders
Paper towels

Directions

1. Freeze plastic spiders in the center of ice cubes.

2. Have children form a circle. Then they pass the spider ice cube around trying to melt it in their hands.

3. The kids can melt these cubes quickly, so have a cube per minute ready to go.

   Variation: Use paper cups instead of an ice cube tray to make larger cubes. To do so, fill a cup one-half to three quarters full. Place the spider in the water and freeze it. After freezing tear the paper cup off before you need to use the cube. These larger ice cubes can take up to five minutes to melt in the children's hands.

   Tip: Have paper towels ready to dry some wet hands.

Spitting Spider (K-6)

Supplies
Ball of dark yarn

Directions

1. Have the kids sit in a circle.

2. Hand the first player a ball of black yarn. The child holds the end of the yarn and tosses the ball to another child.

3. The second player holds onto the yarn or wraps it around his wrist, then throws the ball to another child.

4. Continue until all the children have tossed the ball of yarn and a spider web is formed.

   Variation: Each child adds a sentence onto a story that a parent helper starts before giving the ball of yarn to the first player.

Spitting spiders belong to a family of spiders that live in humid, hot areas. The spitting spider shoots silk from its head, aiming at its prey. It can shoot strands of silk that are more than half an inch long.

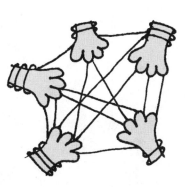

61

Daddy Long Legs (K-6)

Supplies

Version #1
Shoe box
Spider webbing
Three pairs black pantyhose
Nine tennis balls
Version #2
Two shoe boxes
Spider webbing
Six pairs black pantyhose
Eight tennis balls

A daddy long legs is the most well known spider. It is easy to identify because of its long slanted legs, which are white or pale gray. In comparison to its legs, this spider's body is tiny.

Directions

Version #1

1. Take three pairs of black pantyhose and put one tennis ball into each leg, push the balls down into the toe/heel area.

2. Tie the pantyhose around the child's waist allowing the toe/heel area to hit the ground. You now have spider legs — six nylon ones, and the child's own two legs.

3. Place a shoe box without its lid and stand it up on its long edge. Stretch cobwebs over the box's opening. This is your spider web.

4. Now mark a circle on the floor with masking tape. The player stands in the circle, attempting to swing the spider legs and hit a tennis ball (call it a "fly") into the spider web.

5. The tennis balls are placed on the floor within the circle. Use three so each child gets three shots.

6. Players should knock the ball with their make believe spider legs, not their real feet.

Version #2

Daddy Long Legs can also be a great relay game.

1. Form two teams. Attach spider legs to one child on each team. Give each team only one tennis ball (fly), placing the balls in front of each team on the floor.

2. The first teammate swings the legs to knock the fly into the web. (Remember, don't use feet.)

3. Have the player start about five to seven feet back from the spider web.

4. The player retrieves the ball and gives it to the next teammate. A parent helper switches the spider legs from one player to the next and the game continues. Expect lots of laughter. This is hysterical to watch.

5. The first team to finish wins.

Spiders Versus Flies (K-6)

Supplies
Large spider web
Plastic flies
Three plastic spiders

Directions

1. Buy a large pretend spider web such as the kind sold at many grocery and discount department stores at Halloween time.

2. Attach plastic flies to the web.

3. Mark a starting line with masking tape.

4. Have kids take turns tossing three plastic spiders at the web.

5. The object of the game is for the spiders to hook onto the attached flies.

Twisted Spiders (K-6)

Supplies
Twister® game by Milton Bradley®
Music

Directions:

Play Twister® and you'll see how the kids end up looking like tangled spiders.

What makes a school Halloween party fun?

Kari Talbott, 9 years old:
"The decorations make the party fun."

63

Flower Spider Bowling (K-6)

Supplies
Masking tape or cardboard
Three tennis balls

Directions

1. Shape a flower complete with petals on the floor using masking tape or cardboard cut-outs.
2. Mark each petal with a different point score.
3. Designate a starting line with masking tape.
4. The player receives three tennis balls, (pretend these are spiders) to roll onto the flower.
5. The balls need to land on the petals to score.

Spider Crawl (K-2)

Supplies
No materials required

A flower spider is usually found on flowers. While it sits on a flower, the spider's color can change to match the shade of the blossom. Flower spiders capture insects easily because they go unnoticed.

Directions

1. Form two teams.
2. Have the team members stand in a line spreading their legs in a V-pattern.
3. The person at the back of the line gets on the floor pretending to be a spider. The player crawls through the other teammates' legs to reach the front of the line and stands up.
4. The next person at the back of the line continues the same pattern.
5. The first team to complete the spider crawl wins.

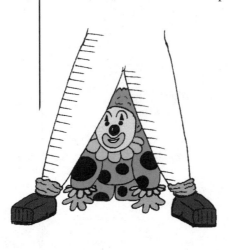

Supplies for Spider Games

Spider Cube Melt (K-6)
Ice cube trays or paper cups
Small plastic spiders
Paper towels

Spitting Spider (K-6)
Ball of black yarn

Daddy Long Legs (K-6)
Version #1
    Shoe box
    Spider webbing
    Three pairs black pantyhose
    Nine tennis balls
Version #2
    Two shoe boxes
    Spider webbing
    Six pairs black pantyhose
    Eight tennis balls

Spider Versus Flies (K-6)
Large spider web
Plastic flies
Three plastic spiders

Twisted Spiders (K-6)
Twister® game by
Milton Bradley®
Music

Flower Spider Bowling (K-6)
Masking tape or cardboard
Three tennis balls

Spider Crawl (K-2)
No materials required

Don't forget the camera and film.

Witch Games

Under the Witch's Broom (K-6)

What makes a school Halloween party fun?

Michelle Ripple, 8 years old:
"The limbo."

Supplies
Pretend witch broom
Cardboard blocks
Halloween music

Directions

1. This is a version of the popular musical game "Limbo," in which players test their flexibility by leaning backward and shimmying under a broomstick or other bar.

2. Use a pretend witch broom as the limbo bar and have the children pass under it.

3. Use cardboard blocks to hold up the broom. These work well because you can lower the blocks for each new round. Or if you have enough helpers, they can hold the broom.

4. Always use music.

Witch's Hat Toss (K-6)

Supplies
Witch hat
Chenille sticks (also called pipe cleaners)
Masking tape

"Witch" means wise one. It is taken from the word "wica."

Directions

1. Before the party, form three rings from chenille sticks that are big enough to fit over the point of a witch's hat.

2. Stand up a witch's hat on the floor or on a table. If necessary, stuff the hat with paper to help it stand better.

3. Using masking tape, make a line on the floor about three feet from the hat.

4. Give the children the three rings and have them toss them at the witches hat to land over the point.

5. Move the line closer to the hat for the younger grades.

Broom Sweep (K-6)

Supplies

Two witch brooms
Two witch hats
Crumpled newspaper
Variation: Orange construction cones

Directions

1. Form two teams.

2. Sitting on the floor in front of them, each team will have a wad of crumpled newspaper, a witch broom, and a witch hat.

3. Place a student's desk about eight feet in front of each team.

4. When a parent helper says "go," the first member of each team puts the witch hat on and sweeps the wad of paper toward and around the desk and back to the team.

5. The next person is handed all of the equipment and proceeds like the first person.

6. The winner is the first team to finish.

7. You can also play the game with a time limit. This might allow some members to go two or three times.

   Variation: Use orange construction cones. Have the teams wind in and out of the cones while sweeping the paper. This version is great for the older grades.

Pass The Broom (K-6)

Supplies

Witch broom
Halloween music
Variation: One broom per four kids

Directions

1. Have the children form a circle and pass the broom around the circle.

2. Play music, then stop it unexpectedly.

3. The person holding the broom has been poisoned by the wicked witch and is out.

4. Start the music again and repeat the process.

5. Keep playing until one child is left.

6. Children who have been eliminated should stand outside the circle and cheer for the others.

   Variation: For older kids pass around several brooms, approximately one per four students. Be sure to play their music. To really confuse them, pass the brooms in alternating directions.

Halloween School Parties:

In William Shakespeare's play Macbeth the three witches chant the following words:

Double, double, toil and trouble;
Fire burn, and cauldron bubble.

Cast A Spell (K-6)

Supplies

Cauldron-type pot
One plastic snake
One plastic frog
One plastic finger
One old rag
Two plastic mice
Three plastic bats
Three plastic toes
Four plastic worms
Five plastic bugs
Poster board

Directions

1. Before the party write the following lists on poster board and display them near the cauldron.

List 1	List 2	List 3
1 Frog	1 Snake	3 Bat
5 Bugs	2 Mice	3 Toes
1 Finger	4 Worms	1 Old Rag

2. Tell the kids that in order for the witch's spell to work the following combination of items need to be tossed into the pot.

3. Mark a starting line.

4. The children choose a list and toss the items from that list into the cauldron trying to cast a spell.

Flying Witches (K-6)

Supplies

Cardboard or plywood
Paints
Notebook paper

Directions

1. Cut a witch shape out of plywood or cardboard. Paint it.

2. Cut out a hole in the stomach area.

3. During the party, have the kids make paper airplanes (pretend they are witches on broomsticks).

4. Have the kids fly their airplanes (witches) through the opening.

Witch Tic-Tac-Toe (K-6)

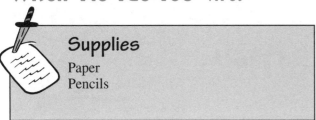

Supplies
Paper
Pencils

Directions

1. Hand out sheets of paper divided into nine boxes.

2. Write this sentence on the chalk board: "Don't be afraid of witches you see on Halloween."

3. Have the children write one word from this sentence into each of their boxes, anywhere they would like, but each word can only be written once.

4. Before the party, write the sentence on a long piece of paper, then clip each word apart so you end up with nine pieces. Put the pieces in a deep bowl.

5. Pull out a piece of paper and read the word. The kids cross off that word on their paper.

6. The first child to cross off three words in a row either across, down or diagonally wins. A few might win simultaneously.

Other examples of nine-word sentences you might use are:

1. Beware of the witch's brew at the witching hour.

2. Why do witches have huge warts on their noses?

3. The witch flies on her broom on Halloween night.

What makes a school Halloween party fun?

Kori Talbott, 8 years old:
"The games."

Megan Knight, 9 years old:
"The games."

Nick Ripple, 11 years old:
"The games."

Supplies for Witch Games

Under the Witch's Broom (K-6)

Pretend witch broom
Cardboard blocks
Halloween music

Witch's Hat Toss (K-6)

Witch hat
Chenille sticks (also called
  pipe cleaners)
Masking tape

Broom Sweep (K-6)

Two witch brooms
Two witch hats
Crumpled newspaper
Variation: Orange construction
  cones

Pass the Broom (K-6)

Witch broom
Halloween music
Variation: One broom per four kids

Cast a Spell (K-6)

Cauldron-type pot
One plastic snake
One plastic frog
One plastic finger
One old rag
Two plastic mice
Three plastic bats
Three plastic toes
Four plastic worms
Five plastic bugs
Poster board

Flying Witches (K-6)

Cardboard or plywood
Paints
Notebook paper

Witch Tic-Tac-Toe (K-6)

Paper
Pencils

Don't forget the camera and film.

All Time Favorite Games

These games do not have a specific theme but are included in the book because of their popularity.

Thumb-Print Art (K-6)

Supplies

Tag board cut into 3" x 4" rectangles
  (one per child)
Stamp pads (orange and/or black)
Markers
Wet towel or wipes

Directions

1. Children make imprints of their thumbs using a stamp pad and placing their thumb-print on pre-cut tag board. have the kids use a wet towl or wipes to clean their thumb.

2. Parent helpers or the kids themselves can turn their thumb prints into black cats, witches, spiders or pumpkins.

3. Using markers personalize the art with the child's name. A parent helper can add scenery such as a witch's broom before the party starts. At party time the child would only need to put their thumb imprint in the appropriate place.

4. Use an orange stamp pad for pumpkin thumb prints and a black pad for the rest of the ideas.

5. Thumb print art is a great take-home favor. A great resource book is: *Ed Emberley's Halloween Drawing Book* by Edward R. Emberley.

Monster Freeze (K-6)

Supplies

Halloween music

Directions

1. Play music from any of your favorite Halloween songs.

2. The kids dance, but when you stop the music they must freeze.

3. Players are eliminated from the game if they move while they should be in a monster freeze pose.

71

Trick or Treat (K-6)

Supplies

Two plastic pumpkins
Plastic baggies/ties
Vegetables such as: Broccoli, cauli-
    flower, zucchini
Halloween candy and trinkets
Paper

Directions

1. Fill a plastic pumpkin with typical Halloween goodies and some not so favorite "treats" such as baggies filled with small servings of raw broccoli, cauliflower, and zucchini.

2. Fill another pumpkin with tricks that the kids can choose, such as: "Spell your name backwards"; "Do ten push-ups"; "crawl on the floor like an alligator."

3. A player picks a trick out of the pumpkin. If the player refuses to do that trick, he must choose a treat (or what he thinks is a treat).

4. The next player takes a turn.

5. Once the kids catch on to what some of the treats are they might all opt to do the tricks.

6. To really surprise the kids, wrap the treats and tell everyone to wait to open them after all the players have taken turns. Explain that some of the treats might be "trick" treats and some will be goodies.

Haunted House (4-6)

Supplies

Will depend on the ideas your parent
    helpers develop

Directions

1. Combine the older classes for a walk through a haunted house that parents make.

2. Use the gym or auditorium.

3. The haunted house takes some preparation by the parents but makes a nice change for the older classes. Two great resource books are:

    1. *How to Haunt a House for Halloween,* by Robert Friedhoffer.

    2. *How to Haunt a House,* by Dan Witkowski

Tombstone Musical Chairs (K-6)

Supplies

Cardboard
Music
Paint or markers
Chairs

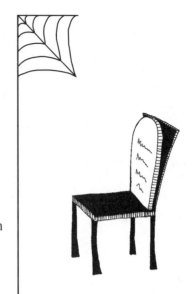

Directions

1. Play this game like the elimination game of musical chairs, but place tombstone shapes cut from cardboard on the back of the chairs. You can use some of the examples found in this section for your epitaphs.

Here I lie for no wonder I am dead, for the wheel of a wagon went over my head.

Soon ripe, soon rotten, soon gone, but not forgotten

I told you I was sick.

Here lies Al, because he messed with a gal.

What I spent I had, what I gave I have, what I saved I lost.

Here lies Mark, because he tried to eat bark.

Anita Nu Life

When your razor is dull and you want to shave, think of the man that lies in this grave.

Here lies my wife, here let her lie. She's at rest and so am I.

Some have children, some have none; here lies the mother of twenty-one.

Here lies a man who did no good, and if he'd lived he never would; where he's gone or how he fares, nobody knows and nobody cares.

Here lies Ben, because he fought with a hen.

73

Mummy Wrap (K-6)

What makes a school Halloween party fun?

Jessica Hoskins, 9 years old:
"Wrapping the teacher up to look like a mummy."

Supplies
Roll of toilet paper (one per child)

Directions

1. Pair up the kids. One person will be the mummy and the other will be the wrapper.

2. The wrappers are each given a roll of toilet paper. On the word "go", they wrap their partners from head to toe leaving the eyes, nose, and mouth uncovered.

3. When the toilet paper runs out or when each child feels he has completed the job, the game is over.

4. The parent helpers check each mummy for completeness and then have the wrappers unwrap their mummies.

5. The first team unwrapped is the winner.

6. Beware there will be lots of toilet paper all over. Make sure to have extra trash bags.

8. Allow about five minutes per wrap. Don't forget to wrap the teacher and take pictures.

Note: Request that each child bring a roll of toilet paper into school the week before the party. This way you can play the game twice. Each child will get to be a mummy and a wrapper.

Tip: If you play this game before you eat, you can use the toilet paper to wipe dirty hands and mouths.

Hidden Halloween Words (1-6)

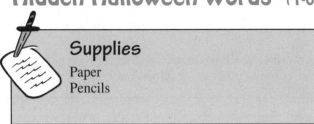

Supplies
Paper
Pencils

Directions

1. The object is to create as many words as possible out of the word "Halloween" or another word related to the holiday.

2. You can only use the letters as many times as they appear in the word Halloween. For example, the letters "l" and "e" in the word Halloween can be used twice, all of the others only once. 3. Set a five-minute time limit.

Eerie Halloween Sounds (K-6)

Supplies
Tape recorder
Cassette tapes

Directions

1. At the beginning of the party, tape record the children making as many eerie Halloween sounds as they can. Play the tape back during refreshment time.

2. Have a parent make copies of the tape for each child. Let the kids know, that when the parent helper has them made, they will be given to them as a Halloween favor.

3. Write the date and year on the tape as a special memory to be saved.

Halloween Word Search (1-6)

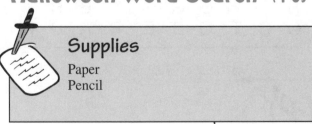

Supplies
Paper
Pencil

Directions

1. Copy the word search (one per student) page 76.

2. Allow approximately 10 minutes to find as many answers as possible

Note: Have this word search on hand in case needed. If it is not used during party time sent it home with the children to be done later.

Halloween

low
lean
no
now
how
an
a
hall
law
hen
all
neal

75

Halloween School Parties:

1. Bat
2. Beware
3. Black
4. Boo
5. Bones
6. Brew
7. Cats
8. Candy
9. Candy Apple
10. Cauldron
11. Cold
12. Cornstalk
13. Costume
14. Creepy
15. Dark
16. Devil
17. Dracula
18. Foggy
19. Frankenstein
20. Fun
21. Games
22. Ghost
23. Goblin
24. Halloween
25. Haunted House
26. Jack O Lantern
27. Monsters
28. Moon
29. Mummies
30. Mummy Wrap
31. October
32. Orange
33. Owl
34. Party
35. Pumpkin
36. Pumpkin Patch
37. Pumpkin Seeds
38. R I P
39. Scary
40. Skeleton
41. Skull
42. Spider
43. Spooky
44. Tombstone
45. Trick or Treat
46. Vampire
47. Web
48. Werewolves
49. Witches
50. Witch Broom

Halloween Word Search (1-6)

Directions

There are 50 hidden words. Search for them. They might be spelled forward, backward, diagonally up or down. Good Luck!

```
V A M P I R E Q S T H N A R B
S C P U M P K I N P A T C H T
D A J F A G G Y S F U F U N O
E N A B O B C D E G N H B X M
E D C G A M E S N J T I R O B
S Y K K H L M N O T E L E K S
N A O S L O U I B J D W W T O
I P L A A P S E N V H N S R N
K P A Y C R O T H N O O M I E
P L N D Q S W S K N U R U C R
M E T N C Z K N E L S D M K E
U S E A M A V E S W E L M O K
P I R C C R W K K O I U I R C
W Y N X O O B N S R L A E T A
D E V I L L C A T S Y C S R L
V R Q L D U S R O B K S W E B
S J A C M S I F O P O R I A B
K H N O R A N G E Z O E T T S
L P I L L U K S E R P T C O Z
A A L T W I T C H E S S H Z V
T R B K R A D T N D B N B A L
S W O I N T Y A O I S O R L O
N Y G W O L P B M P K M O U W
R M E R A W E B B S S P O C E
O M I H H C E P A R T Y M A R
C U P C M R R F O G G Y B R B
E M U T S O C T O B E R A D W
```

76

Supplies for All Time Favorites

Thumb-Print Art (K-6)

Tag board cut into 3" x 4" rectangles
   (one per child)
Stamp pads (orange and/or black)
Markers
Wet towel or wipes

Monster Freeze (K-6)

Halloween music

Trick or Treat (K-6)

Two plastic pumpkins
Plastic baggies/ties
Vegetables such as: Broccoli, cauli-
   flower, zucchini
Halloween candy and trinkets
Paper

Haunted House (4-6)

Will depend on the ideas your parent
   helpers develop

Tombstone Musical Chairs (K-6)

Cardboard
Music
Paint or markers
Chairs

Mummy Wrap (K-6)

Roll of toilet paper (one per child)

Hidden Halloween Words (1-6)

Paper
Pencils

Eerie Halloween Sounds (K-6)

Tape recorder
Cassette tapes

Halloween Word Search (1-6)

Paper
Pencil

Don't forget the camera and film.

CHAPTER THREE
Crafts & Favors

Helpful Hints for Crafts & Favors

1. Many of the items in this chapter call for covered wire. If you can't find it, use bristles from your household broom.

2. Some of the craft ideas in this section can be used in place of a game at one of your activity stations. If you choose an item that needs time to dry leave them at the station. Pass them out before it's time to go home. Make sure to label each one with its owner's name.

3. A lot of the ideas in this section can be interchanged among themes. Example, the painted Frankenstein pot on page 94 can be made into a painted pumpkin pot.

4. If you choose to make some of these crafts at home, or an adult will do the gluing at school you may choose to use a glue gun. It will save time. If children do the craft at school use school glue.

5. Use extreme care if using a glue gun

6. Children have different levels of ability. One child might hurry through a craft while another might need more time to complete the craft.

7. Be prepared with all supplies and directions.

8. Have a finished example of the craft to show the children.

9. Ask children to stop working on their craft and listen if you want to emphasize a point. Children will comprehend directions better if you tell the directions before they begin working on their craft.

10. Try to have one parent helper for every four children in younger grades. And, one parent helper for up to eight older students.

11. Encourage the children to be creative.

12. Try to spend time helping each child when working on a craft.

13. Praise children when they are done with their craft.

14. Allow approximately fifteen minutes for most of the crafts in this chapter.

15. A chenille stem is also called a pipe cleaner.

Bat Favors

Paper Twist Bat (K-6)

Supplies
9" x 8$\frac{1}{2}$" black paper twist (found at craft stores)
2$\frac{3}{8}$" x 1$\frac{7}{8}$" styrofoam egg (found at craft stores)
Glow-in-the-dark fabric paint (white and orange)
2" x 2" black felt
Black yarn or heavy black thread
Tacky glue • Scissors

Directions

1. Make a tube from the paper twist. To do so, unfold the paper twist, then flatten and smooth it with your hands. You may use either side as the right or wrong side but make sure colors are the same. There can be slight variations from both sides.

2. Glue the 9" sides together overlapping by about $\frac{1}{4}$ inch. Let dry.

3. About five to ten minutes after drying, flatten the tube and scallop the ends (pinking shears work well to create a jagged bat-wing look).

4. Place the egg inside and in the middle of the twist tube. Squeeze the tube closed on both sides of the egg and tie with black yarn. Cut off excess yarn. Be careful not to let the egg slide out one end of the tube when tying a knot on the other end.

5. Using glow-in-the-dark fabric paint, paint the eyes and mouth white, and the nose orange. Let it dry.

6. On black felt, trace ears from the pattern shown here. Cut out the ears and glue them onto the bat head. If you would like to hang the bat, attach a piece of black yarn to the head.

EAR PATTERN

Bat Pencil Topper (K-6)

Supplies
Pencil, black if available
Pencil eraser cap
Black permanent ink marker
2" x 1" black poster board
Two 4 mm moving eyes
Glue • Scissors

Directions

1. Make a small ($\frac{1}{4}$") slit in the middle of the eraser cap.

2. Paint the eraser black with the permanent marker and let it dry.

3. Using the pattern, cut bat wings out of the black poster board.

4. Glue the wings to the back of the eraser. Finally, glue on the moving eyes.

Paper Tube Bat (K-6)

Supplies

Toilet paper tube
Black poster board
White and black paint
Two 3 mm red pom-poms
Glue
Scissors

Directions

1. Paint the tube black. Let it dry.

2. Cut ears, legs, and wings out of black poster board using the patterns.

3. Accordion-fold the board to be used for the legs. Then glue the legs onto the bottom edge of the tube.

4. Fold each ear as indicated on the pattern, gluing the ears on the middle of the tube with folded edge down. Hold for a few seconds.

5. Make two $1/2$ " slits opposite each other at both open ends of the tube. Slide the wings into this area and secure with glue if needed.

6. Using white paint make a $1/4$" round circle for the eyes. Let it dry.

7. Glue pom-poms on to the white eyes.

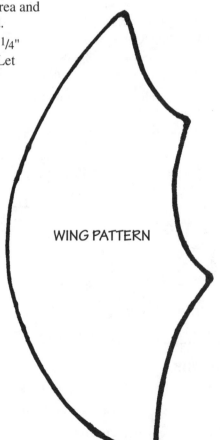

WING PATTERN

LEGS PATTERN

EAR PATTERN

82

Magnificent Bat Magnet (K-6)

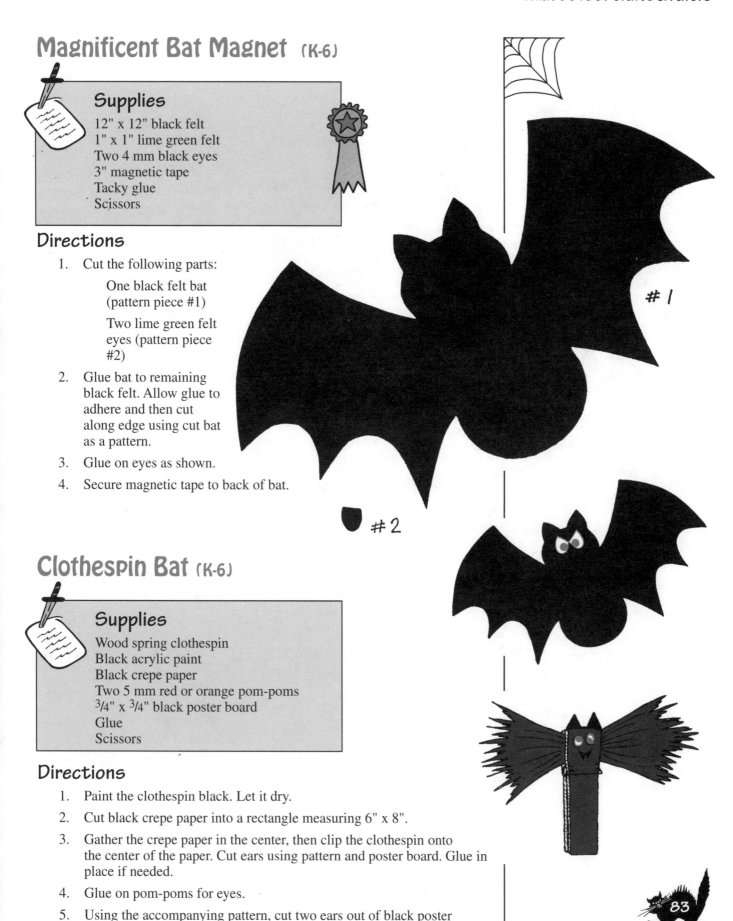

Supplies

12" x 12" black felt
1" x 1" lime green felt
Two 4 mm black eyes
3" magnetic tape
Tacky glue
Scissors

Directions

1. Cut the following parts:

   One black felt bat (pattern piece #1)

   Two lime green felt eyes (pattern piece #2)

2. Glue bat to remaining black felt. Allow glue to adhere and then cut along edge using cut bat as a pattern.

3. Glue on eyes as shown.

4. Secure magnetic tape to back of bat.

Clothespin Bat (K-6)

Supplies

Wood spring clothespin
Black acrylic paint
Black crepe paper
Two 5 mm red or orange pom-poms
$^3/_4$" x $^3/_4$" black poster board
Glue
Scissors

Directions

1. Paint the clothespin black. Let it dry.

2. Cut black crepe paper into a rectangle measuring 6" x 8".

3. Gather the crepe paper in the center, then clip the clothespin onto the center of the paper. Cut ears using pattern and poster board. Glue in place if needed.

4. Glue on pom-poms for eyes.

5. Using the accompanying pattern, cut two ears out of black poster board and glue on to the top of the clothespin.

83

Coney Cousin Bat (K-6)

Supplies

4" styrofoam cone
9" x 12" black craft foam
9" x 9" black felt
2" x 2" lime green felt
3" x 3" black felt
2¹/₂" black pom-pom
Two 1¹/₂" black pom-poms
Two ¹/₄" black pom-poms
Two 5 mm black pom-poms
Three ³/₄" orange pom-poms
Tacky glue • Scissors

Directions

1. Cut the following parts:
   One black felt body (pattern piece #1)
   Two black felt legs (pattern piece #2)

2. Spread glue on bottom of cone and place onto 3" x 3" square of black felt. Trim off excess felt close to the bottom edge of the cone.

3. Place a fine line of glue on one of the straight edges of the cut body piece #1. Place cone on glued edge and roll up tightly. The material will wrap around the cone. Place another line of glue on the overlapping edge of cut body piece and continue to roll to seal. Trim off any excess fabric from the top and the bottom of the cone.

4. Glue 2¹/₂" black pom-pom head on covered body. To glue it correctly, first separate the fluff until you find the center of the pom-pom. Put glue on the top of the cone. Place the top of the cone in the center of the pom-pom and close the pom-pom over the cone. Allow it to dry.

5. Glue the 1¹/₂" pom-pom on legs. Follow directions as in step # 4 for separating the fluff of the pom-poms. Insert the leg strip containing a thin line of glue on one end of the leg strip. Close the pom-pom over the strip.

6. Cut the remaining parts:

Amount	Piece	Pattern	Color/Fabric
Two	Ears	# 3	Black Foam
Two	Eyes	# 4	Green Felt
Two	Wings	# 5	Black Foam
One	Ghost	# 6	White Felt
One	Stem	# 7	Green Felt

7. Separate the fluff on head pom-pom, insert and glue in ears. Close fluff and make sure ears are secure with pressure.

8. Glue on eyes as shown.

9. Apply glue to flat sides of wings and place on sides of body. (Lay bat flat in between two books so the wings are level with the side of the body) Allow the bat to dry fully.

10. Glue the ghost and pumpkins to body as shown.

11. To glue the legs to the body, place legs on a flat surface in a slight upside down V. Apply one inch of glue at the ends of strips where there are no pom-poms. Center the bottom of the body on top of the glued legs and apply pressure.

84

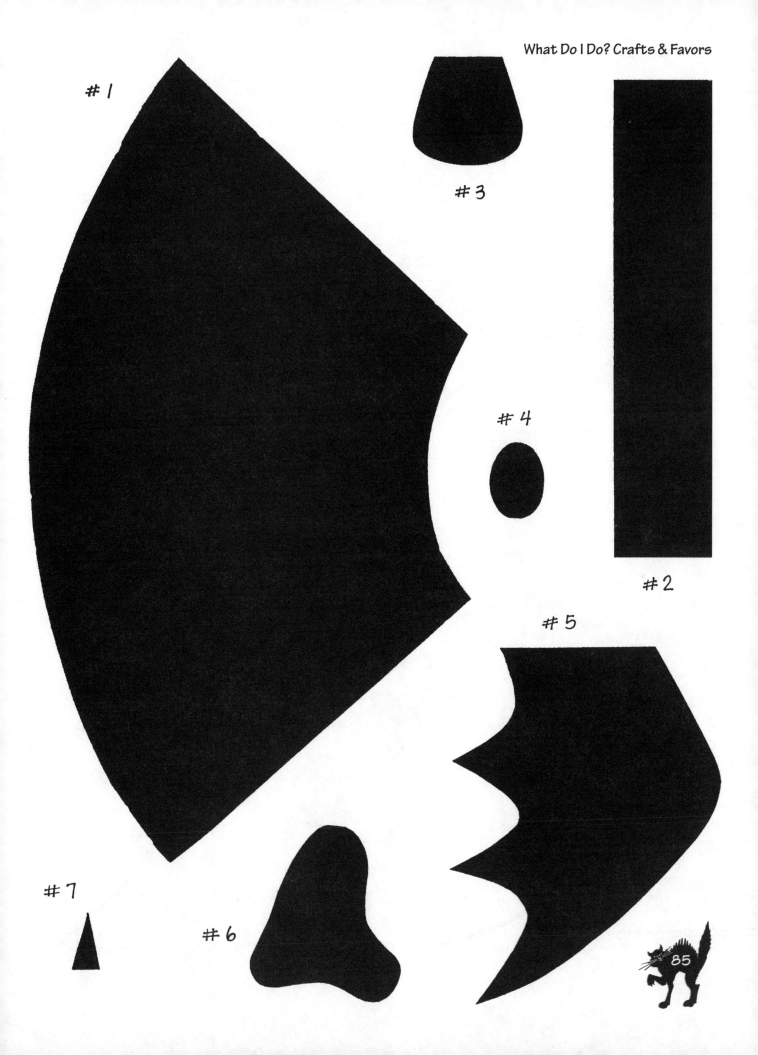

#1

#3

#2

#4

#5

#7

#6

85

Hanger Bat (K-6)

Supplies

Wire hanger
12" x 17" black poster board
Yellow construction paper
  or
Yellow self-adhesive circle labels
12" or 18" black yarn
Glue
Scissors

Directions

1. Lay hanger down on black poster board. Trace around all three sides and then add a cutting margin of $1/2$" all around. Cut out your pattern making sure to scallop the bottom to look like bat wings. Make a copy for the other side of the bat.

2. Trace and cut two bat heads using the pattern here.

3. Glue the hanger-shaped pieces back to back with the hanger in between. Glue the head onto that piece, back to back.

4. Attach bat eyes to face. Make them out of yellow construction paper or self-adhesive circle labels. Tie black yarn to the curve handle to display.

Supplies for Bat Favors

Paper Twist Bat (K-6)
9" x 8 1/2" black paper twist (found at craft stores)
2 3/8" x 1 7/8" styrofoam egg (found at craft stores)
Glow-in-the-dark fabric paint (white and orange)
2" x 2" black felt
Black yarn or heavy black thread
Tacky glue
Scissors

Bat Pencil Topper (K-6)
Pencil, black if available
Pencil eraser cap
Black permanent ink marker
2" x 1" black poster board
Two 4 mm moving eyes
Glue
Scissors

Paper Tube Bat (K-6)
Toilet Paper tube
Black poster board
White and black paint
Two 3 mm red pom-poms
Glue
Scissors

Magnificent Bat Magnet (K-6)
12" x 12" black felt
1" x 1" lime green felt
Two 4 mm black eyes
3" magnetic tape
Tacky glue
Scissors

Clothespin Bat (K-6)
Wood spring clothespin
Black acrylic paint
Black crepe paper
Two 5 mm red or orange pom-poms
3/4" x 3/4" black poster board
Glue
Scissors

Coney Cousin Bat (K-6)
4" styrofoam cone.
9" x 12" black craft foam
9" x 9" black felt
2" x 2" lime green felt
3" x 3" black felt
One 2 1/2" black pom-pom
Two 1 1/2" black pom-poms
Two 1/4" black pom-poms
Two 5 mm black pom-poms
Three 3/4" orange pom-poms
Tacky glue
Scissors

Hanger Bat (K-6)
Wire hanger
12" x 17" black poster board
Yellow construction paper
   or
Yellow self-adhesive circle labels
   12" or 18" black yarn
Glue
Scissors

Cat Favors

Cat Bookmark (K-6)

NOSE PATTERN

Supplies

8" x 2" black felt (body)
1" x 1" white felt (eyes)
1" x 1" lime green felt (nose)
Two 10 mm moving eyes
15 inches of black covered wire, cut into
 2 1/2" lengths (whiskers)
2" black covered wire (mouth)
8" x 2" poster board, any color
Tacky glue
Scissors

Directions

1. Trace the accompanying pattern piece onto black felt and cut out.

2. Cut out the nose from lime green felt. Glue nose in place.

3. Glue on moving eyes.

4. Glue on whiskers and mouth.

   Optional: If you would like to make the bookmark heavier add a thin piece of poster board to the back and trim to fit the shape of the felt.

Cat Rock Paperweight (K-6)

Supplies

3" grey rock
2" square grey felt
Two 12 mm moving eyes
9" grey covered wire or craft whiskers
1/2" grey pom-pom
Tacky glue
Scissors

Directions

1. Wash and dry the rock.

2. Trace and cut ears out of the grey felt. Glue them onto the rock.

3. Glue the moving eyes to the rock.

4. Cut the whiskers into 6 1 1/2" sections. Glue them onto the rock covering the center of the whiskers with the grey pom-pom (nose).

EAR PATTERN

88

Cat Books (K-6)

Supplies

Used books about cats
Black curling ribbon
Orange curling ribbon
Scissors

Directions

1. Shop for cat books at used bookstores or garage sales. Anything will work: Cat cartoons, how-to books about taking care of your cat, or cat stories. Depending on how many books you find, each child can have one or two.

2. Tie books with black and orange curling ribbon and curl lots of ribbon for the top.

Cat Stick Magnet (K-4)

Supplies

Large craft stick
One 2" black pom-pom
2" x 2" black felt
12" black covered wire
5" strip magnetic tape
Two 8 mm moving eyes
Two 3/4" black pom-poms
One black pom-pom for nose
5" Chenille stem (pipe cleaner)
Tacky glue
Scissors

EAR PATTERN

Directions

1. Cut black covered wire into six 2" sections. These are the whiskers.

2. Glue a 2" black pom-pom on the top of a large craft stick.

3. Glue two 3/4" black pom-poms below the large pom-poms to form the cat's front paws.

4. Cut ears out of black felt using the pattern, then glue the ears on the head.

5. Glue eyes, nose, and whiskers onto face.

6. Add the chenille stem (tail), bending it to give it a light curve and gluing it to the back of the craft stem at the top behind the head so the stick stands up straight.

7. Glue magnetic strip on the back of the large craft stick.

89

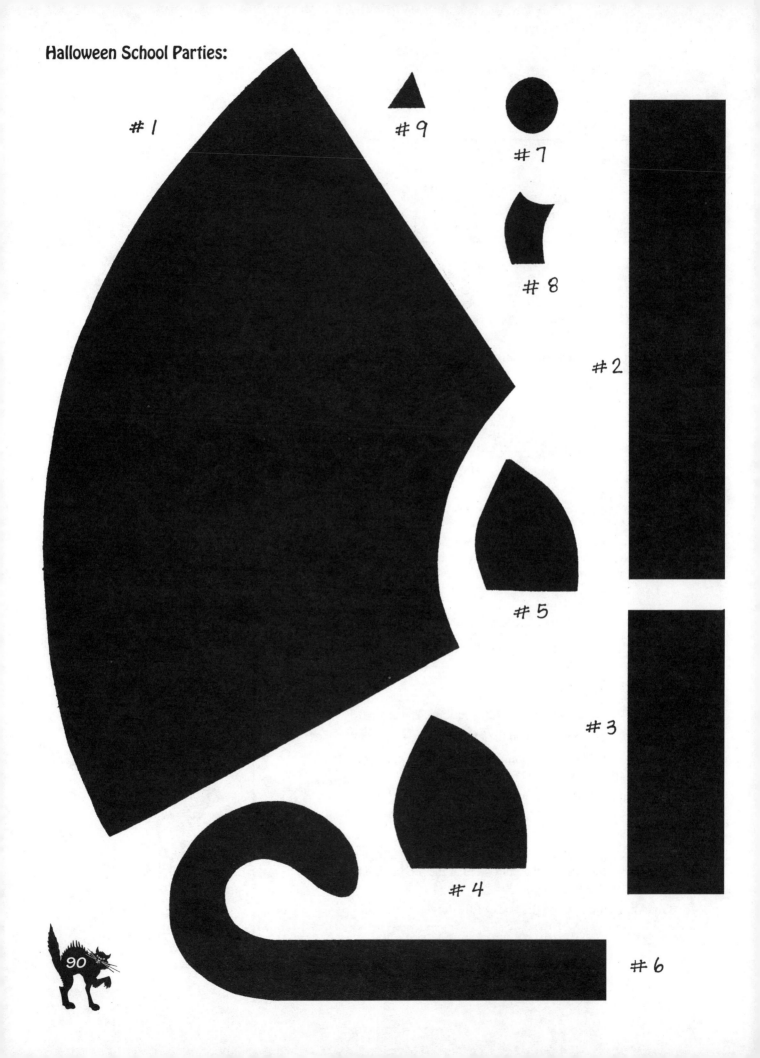

Halloween School Parties:

#1

#9

#7

#8

#2

#5

#3

#4

#6

90

Chenille Cat (K-6)

Supplies

Three black chenille stems
(pipe cleaners)
1" black pom-pom (head)
2" square of black felt (ears)
Two 5 mm moving eyes
6" piece of black covered wire
5 mm black pom-pom (nose)
8 inches of $\frac{1}{8}$" wide orange ribbon
Pin clasp
Tacky glue • Scissors

Directions

1. Twist three black chenille stems together into a cat shape as shown in the picture.

2. Glue on the pom-pom for the head.

3. Cut cat ears out of felt and glue onto pom-pom head.

4. Glue moving eyes onto pom-pom.

5. To make whiskers, cut black wire into six 1" sections and glue onto the pom-pom face.

7. Glue the nose on top of the whiskers.

8. Tie the ribbon around the neck and into a bow.

9. Glue the pin clasp to the back of the chenille stem.

Halloween Cat (K-6)

Supplies

4" styrofoam cone
9" x 12" black felt
3" x 3" orange felt
2" x 2" green felt
$2\frac{1}{2}$" black pom-pom
Four $1\frac{1}{2}$" black pom-poms
3/4" orange pom-pom
Two $\frac{1}{2}$" black pom-poms
$1\frac{1}{2}$" orange pom-pom
9" black covered wire
9" ribbon
Tacky glue • Scissors

Directions

1. Cut the following parts: *Patterns on page 90.*
   One black felt body (pattern piece #1)
   Two black felt legs (pattern piece #2)
   Two black felt arms (pattern piece #3)

91

Halloween Cat (Directions continued from page 91)

2. Spread glue on bottom of cone and place on a 3" x 3" square of black felt. Trim off the excess felt close to the bottom edge of the cone.

3. Place a fine line of glue on one of the straight edges of the cut body piece #1. Place cone on glued edge and roll up tightly. The material will wrap around the cone. Place another line of glue on the overlapping edge of cut body piece and continue to roll to seal. Trim off any excess fabric from the top and bottom of the cone.

4. Glue 2$^1/2$" black pom-pom head on covered body. To glue it correctly, first separate the fluff until you find the center of the pom-pom. Put glue on the top of the cone. Place the top of the cone in the center of the pom-pom and close the pom-pom over the cone. Allow it to dry.

5. Glue the 1$^1/2$" pom-pom on one end of each arm and leg. Follow directions as in step # 4 for separating the fluff of the pom-pom. Insert the arm and leg strip containing a thin line of glue on one end of each arm and leg strip. Close the pom-pom over the strips.

6. Cut the remaining parts:

Amount	Piece	Pattern	Color/Fabric
Two	Outer Ear	#4	Black felt
Two	Inner Ear	#5	Orange felt
One	Tail	#6	Black felt
Two	Eyes	#7	Green felt
One	Stem	#8	Green felt
Three	Triangles	#9	Black felt

7. Glue the inner ear to the outer ear.

8. Separate the fluff on head pom-pom and insert and glue in ears. Close fluff and make sure ears are secure with pressure.

9. Cut the wire into three equal lengths. Glue the center of the wires to the underside of the nose pom-pom to form the whiskers. Glue the facial features (nose, whiskers, eyes) on the head pom-pom as shown in picture.

10. Glue the arms to the body, apply glue to the ends of the strips where there are no pom-poms. Lift the head pom-pom fluff away from the neck and place the glued arms under the fluff to the body at the sides of neck.

11. Tie the ribbon in a bow and glue it center front under the chin.

12. Glue the pumpkin pom-pom to the body by pulling the fluff back and laying the center of the pom-pom flat against the body. Glue on three triangles for face, glue on pumpkin stem.

13. Glue the legs to the body, place the legs on a flat surface in a slight upside down V. Apply glue 1" in length from unballed ends of leg strip. Center the bottom of the body on top of the glued legs and apply pressure.

14. Apply glue to the end of the tail and place it next to the edge of the back seam (this will enable the tail to lay to the side).

Supplies for Cat Favors

Cat Bookmark (K-6)

8" x 2" black felt (body)
1" x 1" white felt (eyes)
1" x 1" lime green felt (nose)
Two 10 mm moving eyes
15 inches of black covered wire, cut into 2 1/2" lengths (whiskers)
2" black covered wire (mouth)
8" x 2" poster board, any color
Tacky glue
Scissors

Cat Rock Paperweight (K-6)

3" grey rock
2" square grey felt
Two 12 mm moving eyes
9" grey covered wire or craft whiskers
1/2" grey pom-pom
Tacky glue
Scissors

Cat Books (K-6)

Used books about cats
Black curling ribbon
Orange curling ribbon
Scissors

Cat Stick Magnet (K-4)

Large craft stick
One 2" black pom-pom
2" x 2" black felt
12" black covered wire
5" strip magnetic tape

Two 8 mm moving eyes
Two 3/4" black pom-poms
One black pom-pom for nose
5" chenille stem (pipe cleaner)
Tacky glue
Scissors

Chenille Cat (K-6)

Three black chenille stems (pipe cleaners)
1" black pom-pom (head)
2" square of black felt (ears)
Two 5 mm moving eyes
6" piece of black covered wire
5 mm black pom-pom (nose)
8 inches of 1/8" wide orange ribbon
Pin clasp
Tacky glue
Scissors

Halloween Cat (K-6)

4" styrofoam cone
9" x 12" black felt
3" x 3" orange felt
2" x 2" green felt
2 1/2" black pom-pom
Four 1 1/2" black pom-poms
3/4" orange pom-pom
Two 1/2" black pom-poms
1 1/2" orange pom-pom
9" black covered wire
9" ribbon
Tacky glue
Scissors

Frankenstein Favors

Painted Frankenstein Pot (K-6)

Supplies

Any size clay pot (mini ones make great favors)
Green acrylic paint
Black acrylic paint
Red acrylic paint
Grey acrylic paint
Paintbrush
Two clear push pins
Wire cutters
Metal file
Glue gun
Halloween candies

Directions

1. Paint clay pot Frankenstein green and let it dry.

2. Create a Frankenstein face on the pot with acrylic paints.

3. Paint black hair sticking up all around the top of the pot. Give it a jagged, spiked look.

4. With red paint, make a scar on his forehead and on his lower cheeks.

5. Using wire cutters, cut off the pins from the push pins. Smooth any remaining pin with the metal file.

6. Paint the pin handles grey to look like bolts. Glue them at the neck area.

7. Fill the pot with candies.

Optional: Finish pots with varnish or similar coating.

Frankenstein's Bolt Necklace (K-4)

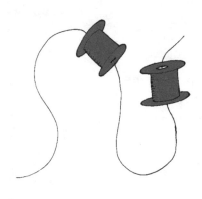

Supplies

1/2"x5/8" wooden spools (found at craft stores)
Green acrylic paint
Macrame cording, green or black
Paintbrush
Scissors

Directions

1. Cut the macrame cording after measuring the childs' neck size and adding additional length to hang properly. Also, allow approximately 6" additional cording for tieing.

2. Paint the wooden spools green. Let the children thread cording through the spools.

Ghoulish Popcorn Hands (K-6)

Supplies

Disposable clear gloves, not powdered
   (purchase at a food store, not a
   beauty supply store)
Candy corn
Popcorn
Green curling ribbon

Directions

1. Fill a disposable clear glove with candy corn in each finger to represent fingernails.

2. Fill the glove with popped popcorn.

3. Tie at the wrist with ribbon.

Frankenstein's Laboratory Hand (1-6)

Supplies

18" x 12" lime green construction paper
Five chenille stems (pipe cleaners)
   any color
Black or red construction paper
Popsicle stick
Plastic spider rings
Glue

Directions

1. Cut the chenille stems in half.

2. Have each child trace a hand (right or left) onto a folded piece of lime green paper.

3. Their wrist needs to be placed at the fold while tracing. Tell them to cut out their hand shapes, but do not cut through the fold.

4. Open up the hand shape.

5. On the inside of the hand, cut to fit and glue a chenille stem onto each finger but only onto one side of the double hand. Let it dry a few minutes.

6. Now glue down the opposite half of the double hand to form a single hand.

7. Cut out fingernails from construction paper and glue them in place. Let the kids choose to have black or red fingernails.

8. Glue a popsicle stick to the bottom edge of the hand at the wrist. Paint the stick red if you use red fingernails and black if you use black fingernails.

9. Because of the chenille sticks the kids can bend their fingers into interesting shapes. Give each child a spider ring to put on a finger.

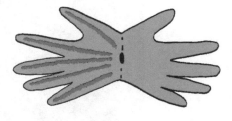

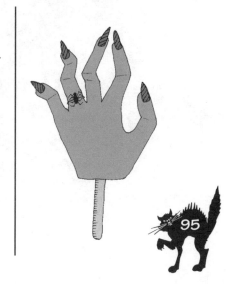

95

Frankenstein Sings (K-6)

Supplies

Empty frozen juice can with lid
   (one per child)
Stones
Beans (uncooked)
Rice (uncooked)
Popcorn kernels
Green construction paper
Two black gumdrops or two small corks
Tape
Markers
Tacky glue
Scissors

Directions

1. Long before the party, start saving empty, clean frozen juice cans complete with the removable lids.

2. Put a mixture of dry beans, rice, small stones, and popcorn kernels into a juice can.

3. Glue the edges of the lid and place on the can. Secure it again by taping the edges of the lid to the edges of the can.

4. Wrap green construction paper around the can, gluing or taping it in place. Stand the can up. This will become Frankensteins's head and neck.

5. Glue black gumdrops or corks opposite each other on the bottom sides of the can. These represent the bolts on Frankenstein's neck. Have the kids use markers to draw his face and scars.

Supplies for Frankenstein Favors

Painted Frankenstein Pot (K-6)

Any size clay pot (mini ones make
  great favors)
Green acrylic paint
Black acrylic paint
Red acrylic paint
Grey acrylic paint
Paintbrush
Two clear push pins
Wire cutters
Metal file
Glue gun
Halloween candies

Frankenstein's Bolt Necklace (K-4)

3/4" wooden spools (found at
  craft stores)
Green acrylic paint
Macrame cording, green or black
Paintbrush
Scissors

Ghoulish Popcorn Hands (K-6)

Disposable clear gloves, not
  powdered (purchase at a food
  store, not a beauty
  supply store)
Candy corn
Popcorn
Green curling ribbon

Frankenstein's Laboratory Hand (1-6)

18" x 12" lime green
  construction paper
Five chenille stems (pipe cleaners)
  any color
Black or red construction paper
Popsicle stick
Plastic spider rings
Glue

Frankenstein Sings (K-6)

Empty frozen juice can with lid
  (one per child)
Stones
Beans (uncooked)
Rice (uncooked)
Popcorn kernels
Green construction paper
Two black gumdrops or two
  small corks
Tape
Markers
Tacky glue
Scissors

Ghost Favors

Ghost Magnet (K-6)

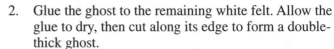

Supplies
12" x 12" white felt
2" x 2" yellow felt
1" x 1" black felt
3" magnetic tape
6" black covered wire
Two 5 mm half beads
Scissors

Directions

1. Cut the following parts from the accompanying patterns:

   White felt ghost (pattern piece #1)

   Two yellow felt eyes (pattern piece #2)

   Two black felt eyes (pattern piece #3)

   Orange nose (pattern piece #4)

2. Glue the ghost to the remaining white felt. Allow the glue to dry, then cut along its edge to form a double-thick ghost.

3. Bend wire to form the mouth.

4. Position and glue on eyes (black bead on top of yellow felt), nose, and mouth as shown.

5. Secure magnetic tape to back of ghost.

1

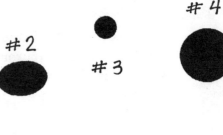

2   # 3   # 4

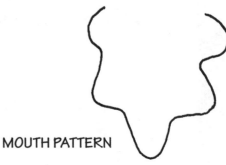

MOUTH PATTERN

Ghost Sucker Card (K-6)

Supplies
5" x 7" white poster board
Flat wrapped orange sucker
Black permanent ink marker
Scissors
Markers

Directions

1. Cut a ghost shape out of poster board.

2. Decorate the ghost with eyes using the marker.

3. Poke two holes in the center of the ghost. With the sucker slide the stick through the holes. The sucker becomes the ghost nose.

Ghost Can (K-6)

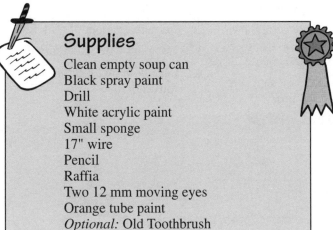

Supplies
Clean empty soup can
Black spray paint
Drill
White acrylic paint
Small sponge
17" wire
Pencil
Raffia
Two 12 mm moving eyes
Orange tube paint
Optional: Old Toothbrush

Directions

1. With black spray paint, paint the outside of the can thoroughly, let it dry.

2. Drill a small hole into both sides of the can near the top.

3. Wind each end of the wire around a pencil, slide it off. Hook each end into the drilled holes on the can bending the wire so it stays secure.

4. Using a sponge dipped into white paint, sponge lightly a ghost shape onto the front of the can.

5. Tie a raffia bow onto the handle.

6. Glue on the eyes.

7. With orange tube paint, write the word BOO near the ghost.

8. Fill the can with assorted treats.

Bubble Ghost (K-6)

Supplies

Version #1	Version #2
Two 8" squares of white felt	Two 8" squares of white felt
Sewing machine	Sewing machine
White thread	White thread
3" square black felt	3" square black felt
Jar of bubbles	Jar of bubbles
Tacky glue	Tacky glue
Scissors	Scissors
	3" covered wire
	2" square of pink felt

Directions

Version #1

1. Trace the pattern and cut two ghost shapes out of white felt.

2. Sew them together, leaving the bottom open. There's no need to turn the ghost inside out.

3. Cut three black 1" circles to glue on for eyes and nose.

4. Slide the felt ghost over a jar of bubbles.

Version #2

1. Follow directions 1-4 as in version #1.

2. Cut a tongue out of pink felt.

3. Form the wire into a mouth.

4. Glue both on as in the illustration.

Flying Ghost (K-6)

Supplies

2" styrofoam ball
24" wire
Straw
18" x 18" white fabric
6" ribbon (any color)
Pinking shears
Black permanent ink marker or black felt

Directions

1. Fold the wire in half and wrap it around a straw. Insert the wire into and through the center of the styrofoam ball. You now have a ghost head and arms.

2. Using pinking shears, pink the edges of the fabric. Drape the fabric over the ball pulling the wire through the fabric.

3. Tie a ribbon around the neck.

4. Using a permanent marker draw facial features on the ghost's head. Or use felt cut into eyes and nose shapes and glue them on the head.

5. Hang from the wire.

100

PATTERN FOR BUBBLE GHOST VERSION #1 AND #2

Ghost Glue Necklace (K-6)

Supplies

White school glue
Wax paper
Paper hole puncher
28" - 32" yarn (any color)
Black permanent ink marker

Directions

1. Squeeze a blob of white glue onto wax paper into a shape of a ghost. Let it dry.

2. Peel the ghost from the wax paper after a day or two. At this time you must punch a hole near the top. Turn it over to allow for additional drying (approximately 1-2 days).

   Note: If the glue has dried too much it will crack the whole ghost.

3. Slide yarn or string through the hole and knot to make a necklace.

4. Draw eyes and a mouth on the ghost with permanent marker.

5. Make a few extras in case some break.

   Optional: Personalize with the childs' name.

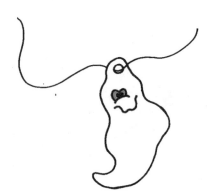

Ghost Sucker (K-6)

Supplies

10" square white fabric
Tootsie Roll Pop® suckers (any flavor)
6" ribbon (any color)
Optional: One large apple

Directions

1. Place the Tootsie Roll Pop® in the center of the fabric. Gather the fabric around the stick just below the ball shaped candy (the ghost's head).

2. Tie a ribbon around the ghost's "neck".

3. Draw ghost eyes on the fabric head with a permanent marker.

   Optional: Stand these ghost suckers up by pushing the sticks into apples.

Supplies for Ghost Favors

Ghost Magnet (K-6)
12" x 12" white felt
2" x 2" yellow felt
1" x 1" black felt
3" magnetic tape
6" black covered wire
Two 5 mm half beads
Scissors

Ghost Sucker Card (K-6)
5" x 7" white poster board
Flat wrapped orange sucker
Black permanent ink marker
Scissors
Markers

Ghost Can (K-6)
Clean empty soup can
Black spray paint
Drill
White acrylic paint
Small sponge
17" wire
Pencil
Raffia
Two 12 mm moving eyes
Orange tube paint
Optional: Old Toothbrush

Bubble Ghost (K-6)
Version #1
    Two 8" squares of white felt
    Sewing machine
    White thread
    3" square black felt
    Jar of bubbles

Tacky glue
Scissors
Version #2
    Two 8" squares of white felt
    Sewing machine
    White thread
    3" square black felt
    Jar of bubbles
    Tacky glue
    Scissors
    3" covered wire
    2" square of pink felt

Flying Ghost (K-6)
2" styrofoam ball
24" wire
Straw
18" x 18" white fabric
6" ribbon (any color)
Pinking shears
Black permanent ink
    marker or black felt

Ghost Glue Necklace (K-4)
White school glue
Wax paper
Paper hole puncher
28" - 32" yarn (any color)
Black permanent ink marker

Ghost Sucker (K-6)
10" square white fabric
Tootsie Roll Pop® suckers
    (any flavor)
6" ribbon (any color)
Optional: One large apple

Pumpkin Favors

Pumpkin Magnet (K-6)

Supplies

9" x 6" orange felt
3" x 3" green felt
2" x 2" brown felt
4" green chenille stem (pipe cleaner)
Two 7 mm moving eyes
2" black covered wire
3" magnetic tape
Rounded toothpick
Tacky glue
Scissors

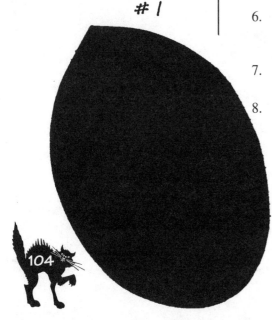

Directions

1. Cut out the following parts:

   Small orange felt pumpkin (pattern piece #1)

   Green felt leaf (pattern piece #2)

   Brown felt stem (pattern piece #3)

   Middle size orange felt pumpkin (pattern piece #4)

   Large orange felt pumpkin (pattern piece #5)

2. Position and glue the stem to the top of the large pumpkin.

3. Apply glue to the middle-size pumpkin piece and keeping centered glue on top of the stem and large pumpkin.

4. Apply glue to the small pumpkin piece and keeping centered glue on top of the middle-size piece.

5. Wrap the chenille stem around a toothpick. Slip it off the toothpick, then bend it slightly to form a vine.

6. Glue one end of the vine to the base of the brown stem. Glue the leaf on as shown. Tack the other end of the vine to the pumpkin using a small amount of glue.

7. Position and glue face on as shown. For the smile, shape the wire first. Spread glue thinly on one side of the wire and then glue as shown.

8. Secure magnetic tape to the back of the pumpkins.

1

2

3

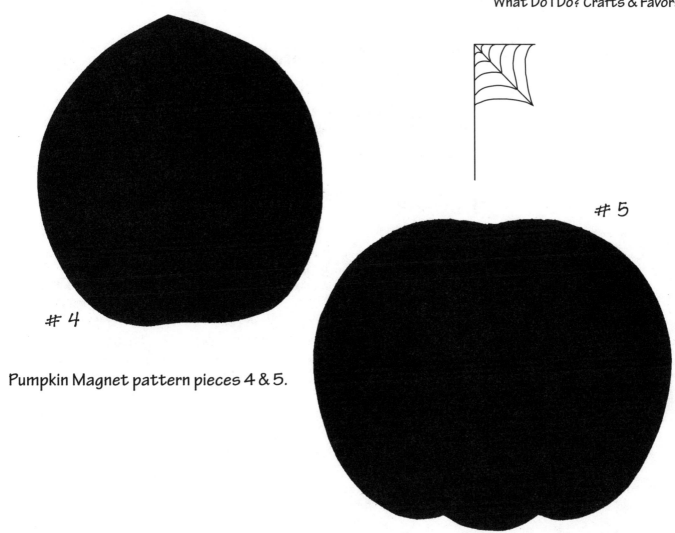

5

4

Pumpkin Magnet pattern pieces 4 & 5.

Mr. Penny Pumpkin (K-1)

Supplies

Seven pennies
Orange poster board
Brown marker
1" square black construction paper
Large craft stick
Hot glue gun or tacky glue

Directions

1. Cut a 5" round circle from orange poster board, adding a 1" square stem on top before cutting.

2. Color the stem brown with the marker.

3. Glue facial features on the pumpkin, using pennies for the eyes, a black paper triangle for the nose, and five pennies for the mouth.

4. Glue the pumpkin onto a large craft stick.

5. Personalize the stick with the child's name.

    Note: Pennies adhere better using a glue gun.

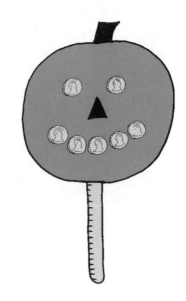

Pumpkin Photo Card (K-6)

Supplies

Polaroid camera and film
8 1/2" x 11" orange construction paper
  (one per student)
Felt pens
Scissors • Glue

Directions

1. Take a picture of each child in costume. If you have someone creative that would like to design a Halloween photo backdrop, it would add to the pictures. You may also want to use a decorated bulletin board for the background. If you don't have access to a Polaroid camera, use a regular camera and have the pictures developed to hand out later.

2. Fold the orange construction paper in half .

3. Draw and cut a pumpkin shape only on one side, making sure it is the right size to display the picture. Make a sample frame before cutting out all your frames.

4. Glue the picture in place, behind the pumpkin opening. Somewhere on the frame, personalize with the student's and teacher's names and the year.

5. On the inside of the card write the names of the students in the order they were seated.

   Tip: To save handwriting time write students name out once, make copies and glue the copies on the inside of the card.

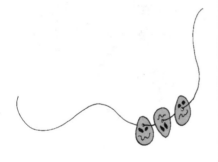

Pumpkin Seed Necklace (K-6)

Supplies

Pumpkin seeds (Fresh from a pumpkin)
White thread
Needle
Optional: Paints or permanent markers

Directions

1. Seeds must be soft. Cut the pumpkin before the party. Wash and pat dry the seeds before the kids start working.

2. Cut the thread long enough for the necklace to fit comfortably over a child's head. Tie a big knot in one end.

3. Have the kids thread one pumpkin seed at a time onto their needles, carefully pushing it to the end of the thread where the knot is. Continue with more seeds.

4. When there are enough seeds on the necklace, tie both ends together.

5. The necklaces can me made ahead of time by parent helpers. The children then can paint the seeds to make their own creations. Paint must dry, so also consider using permanent markers.

Note: One pumpkin has approximately 400 seeds.

Pumpkin Play "Clay" (K-3)

Supplies

1 cup flour
2 teaspoons cream of tarter
1/2 cup salt
1 cup water
1 tablespoon vegetable oil
Orange food coloring
Four sandwich bags
24" green ribbon or yarn
Halloween cookie cutter
Hole puncher

1" x 2" plain white paper
One of the following:
 Black construction
  paper/scissors
 Black felt/scissors
 Black permanent ink
  marker

This recipe makes four pumpkins.

Directions

1. In a sauce pan, combine the flour, cream of tarter, and salt.

2. In a separate container, combine the water, oil, and food coloring.

3. Slowly stir the liquid mixture into the flour mixture.

4. Cook for about 3 minutes over medium heat until the mixture pulls away from the sides of the pan. Cool slightly.

5. Form four balls and place in sandwich baggies. Tie each bag with a 6" piece of green ribbon or yarn. Attach a Halloween cookie cutter to the ribbon along with the "clay" recipe written on paper. Punch a hole in the paper to slide the ribbon through.

6. Using black construction paper or felt, cut out Jack-o-lantern's eyes, a nose, and a mouth to glue onto the outside of the bag. You may opt to draw the face on with black permanent marker.

Pumpkin Candy Jar (K-6)

Supplies

Clear 4" canister.
2" orange pom-pom
4" green chenille stem (pipe cleaner)
2" square black felt
Candy
Tacky glue
Scissors

Directions

1. Glue the orange pom-pom to the lid of the canister.

2. Fold the chenille stem in half once, then fold again and twist. Glue it on top of the pom-pom as the pumpkin stem.

3. Cut eyes, a nose, and a mouth out of black felt and glue onto the pumpkin.

4. Fill the jar with candy.

Supplies for Pumpkin Favors

Pumpkin Magnet (K-6)
9" x 6" orange felt
3" x 3" green felt
2" x 2" brown felt
4" green chenille stem
   (pipe cleaner)
Two 7 mm moving eyes
2" black covered wire
3" magnetic tape
Rounded toothpick
Tacky glue
Scissors

Mr. Penny Pumpkin (K-1)
Seven pennies
Orange poster board
Brown marker
1" square black construction paper
Large craft stick
Hot glue gun or tacky glue

Pumpkin Photo Card (K-6)
Polaroid camera and film
8½" x 11" orange construction
   paper (one per student)
Felt pens
Scissors
Glue

Pumpkin Seed Necklace (K-3)
Pumpkin seeds (Fresh from a
   pumpkin)
White thread
Needle

Optional: Paints or permanent
   markers
Note: One pumpkin has approximately 400 seeds.

Pumpkin Play "Clay" (K-3)
1 cup flour
2 teaspoons cream of tarter
½ cup salt
1 cup water
1 tablespoon vegetable oil
Orange food coloring
Four sandwich bags
24" green ribbon or yarn
Halloween cookie cutter
Hole puncher
1" x 2" plain white paper
One of the following:
   Black construction paper/
   scissors
   Black felt/scissors
   Black permanent ink marker
This recipe makes four pumpkins.

Pumpkin Candy Jar (K-6)
Clear 4" canister.
2" orange pom-pom
4" green chenille stem
   (pipe cleaner)
2" square black felt
Candy
Tacky glue
Scissors

Skeleton Favors

Skeleton Pickup Game (K-6)

Supplies
White twist ties, large roll (available at hardware stores)

Directions

1. This project requires twist ties that are similar to the ones packaged with sandwich and garbage bags. But you'll need a roll that comes packaged with a cutter. This is a good favor to prepare before the party.

2. Use the picture to put together your skeleton.

3. Give each child the following instructions along with six to twelve skeletons.

   To play: Dump all the skeletons on the floor. Pick one skeleton up and try to catch the other skeletons by hooking onto their feet or hands. Have a race with a friend to see who can pick up their skeletons faster.

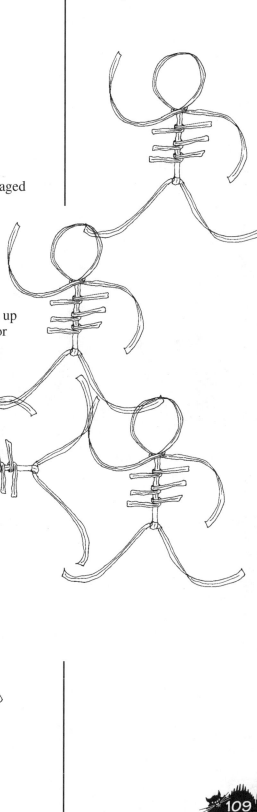

109

Adjoining Skeleton (2-6)

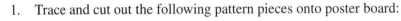

Supplies

White poster board
Black marker
Hole puncher
Crayons or colored markers
Paper fasteners (14 per skeleton)
Kite string
Scissors
Optional: Thread and glow-in-the-dark paints

Directions

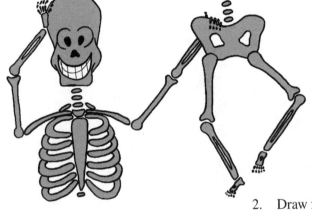

1. Trace and cut out the following pattern pieces onto poster board:

   One head

   One rib cage

   One hip bone

   Two arms (pattern piece #1)

   Two arms (pattern piece #2)

   Two legs (pattern piece #3)

   Two legs (pattern piece #4)

   Two feet

   Two hands

2. Draw facial features and bone markings as shown in the illustration. *Optional:* Use glow-in-the-dark paint if you like.

3. Use a paper hole puncher and punch holes where indicated on the pattern pieces.

4. Color a small area around the punched holes onto the backside of the skeleton using the colors as indicated in the illustrations. Doing so, allows you to connect the skeleton easily. There is no color needed at the top of the head.

5. Attach the same color to the same color using the paper fasteners.

6. Thread a desired length of kite string through the hole in the head to allow the skeleton to be hung.

   Optional: Kite string or thread may be used to attach to the legs or arms to use the skeleton as a puppet.

Tip: I have found that it is best to have this pre-cut and color coded prior to the party. Depending on grade level allow up to 20 minutes if children will assemble.

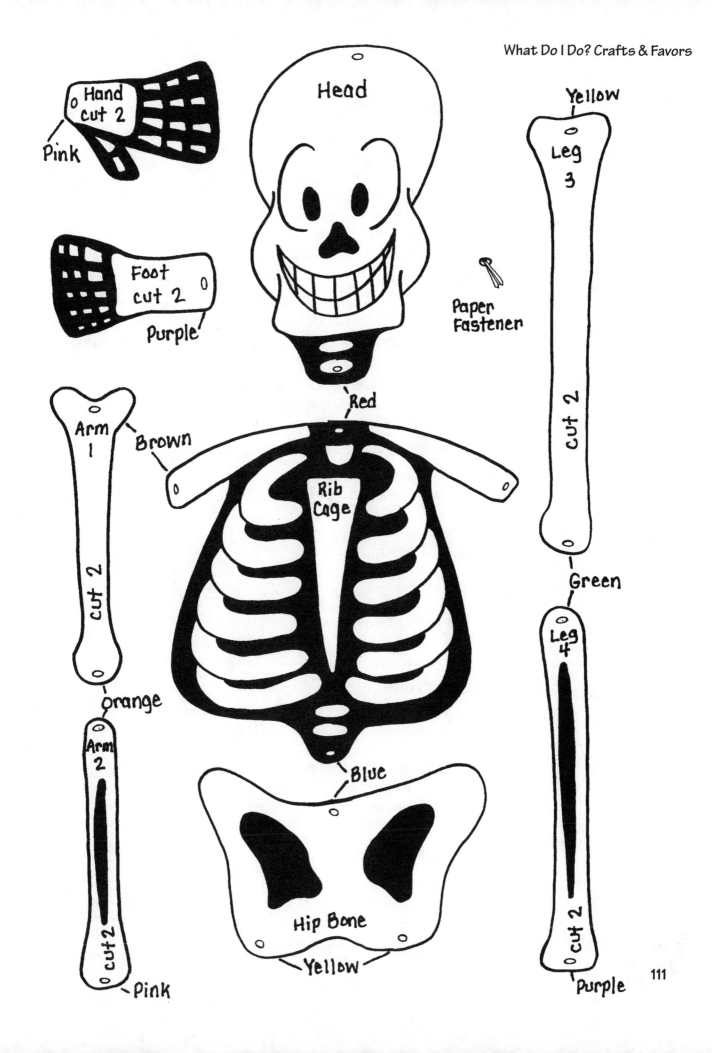

Hand
cut 2

Pink

Foot
cut 2

Purple

Head

Paper
Fastener

Yellow

Leg
3

cut 2

Green

Arm
1

Brown

cut 2

Rib
Cage

Red

Leg
4

cut 2

orange

Arm
2

cut 2

Pink

Blue

Hip Bone

Yellow

Purple

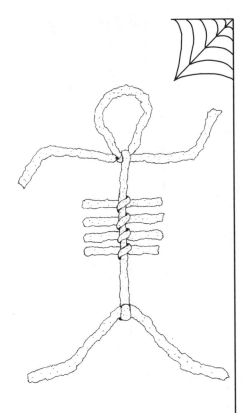

"Fuzzy" Skeleton (K-6)

Supplies

Four 12" long white chenille stems
   (pipe cleaners)
Scissors

Directions:

1. Everyone can bend this fun skeleton into shape using white chenille sticks.

2. The rib bones are made from 3" pieces.

3. The head is made from a 6" piece.

4. The arms are made from a 12" piece.

5. The trunk of the body and the left leg are one piece 12" long.

6. The right leg is 6" long.

7. Connect using the illustration as your guide.

Skeleton Bone Necklace (K-6)

Supplies

Chicken bones (one or more per necklace)
Drill
Macrame cording
32 inches, if you drill a hole in the bones
50 inches, if you wrap it around the bones
Permanent ink markers

Directions

1. Save up chicken bones or ask at your grocery store for leftover bones.

2. Boil them for about 10 minutes to cleanse.

3. If a bone is large enough, drill a small hole in it through which to thread macrame cording. If the bone is small, tie the cording around it a few times to secure.

4. The bones can be painted if you like or permanent marker can be used to personalize them. Use one or more bones per necklace.

Use a clean chicken leg bone or wishbone. Soak it in a container with vinegar overnight. The bigger the bone the more days you let it soak. When you're ready, rinse off the vinegar and you will be able to bend the bones. Why does the vinegar make the bone bendable?

Skeleton Flyer (K-6)

Supplies

Black construction paper
White construction paper
Glue
Scissors

Directions

1. Fold a paper airplane out of black construction paper.

2. Decorate by gluing on bone shapes that are cut out of white construction paper.

3. Kids will zoom by with this favor.

Tombstone Favor Cup (K-6)

Supplies

Two 3" squares x 1" thick styrofoam
Black styrofoam spray paint (found at
    craft stores)
Plain white paper
Small paper nut cup
Spanish moss
Halloween candy or trinkets
Tacky glue

Directions

1. Cut a tombstone shape out of one of the Styrofoam squares. Use the other square for the bottom of the tombstone to sit on.

2. Paint them with black styrofoam spray paint.

3. Draw a skull and crossbones onto the tombstone or write "RIP" on a white piece of paper and glue onto the tombstone.

4. Glue the tombstone to the bottom piece setting the tombstone at the back edge.

5. Spray paint the outside of the nut cup.

6. Glue the nut cup in front of the tombstone on the bottom piece.

7. Place Spanish moss at the base of the tombstone and around the nut cup. Fill with your choice of treats.

Supplies for Skeleton Favors

Skeleton Pickup Game (K-6)
White twist ties, large roll
   (available at hardware stores)

Adjoining Skeleton (2-6)
White poster board
Black marker
Hole puncher
Crayons or colored markers
Paper fasteners
   (14 per skeleton)
Kite string
Scissors
Optional: Thread and glow-in-the-
   dark paints

Fuzzy Skeleton (K-6)
Four 12" long white chenille stems
   (pipe cleaners)
Scissors

Skeleton Bone Necklace (K-4)
Chicken bones (one or more
   per necklace)

Drill
Macrame cording
32 inches, if you drill a hole
   in the bones
50 inches, if you wrap it around
   the bones
Permanent ink markers

Skeleton Flyer (K-6)
Black construction paper
White construction paper
Glue
Scissors

Tombstone Favor Cup (K-6)
Two 3" squares x 1" thick styrofoam
Black styrofoam spray paint (found
   at craft stores)
Plain white paper
Small paper nut cup
Spanish moss
Halloween candy or trinkets
Tacky glue

Spider Favors

Spider Web Plaque (K-6)

Supplies

Version #1

5" x 5" x $\frac{1}{2}$" thick wooden board
Black spray paint
Eight small nails
Bright orange yarn
Plastic spider
Scissors
Hammer

Version #2

$4\frac{1}{2}$" x $4\frac{1}{2}$" black poster board
Twelve to sixteen popsicle sticks
Black spray paint
Eight small nails
Bright orange yarn
Plastic spider
Wood glue
Scissors
Hammer

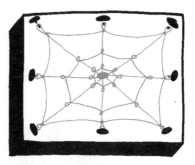

Directions

Version #1

1. Paint the wooden board black.

2. Hammer small nails at each corner and midway between.

3. Tie bright orange yarn from corner to corner and from the center nails to the opposing nails.

4. Form three concentric circles by weaving yarn around your straight strands. Space your circles about $\frac{1}{2}$" apart. A spider web will form.

5. Add a plastic spider if you would like.

Version #2

1. If you have no one to cut the wood for the bases in version #1, then build your base with popsicle sticks and cardboard. Glue a popsicle stick at each end of the $4\frac{1}{2}$" square poster board.

2. Glue the next two sticks to the ends of the first two sticks.

3. Keep layering your sticks alternately until you reach a height that will hold your nail size.

4. Spray this base with black paint, then continue at step 2 of version #1.

Spider Magnet (K-6)

Supplies

5" x 6" black felt
1" x 1" orange felt
2" x 2" white felt
Three 12" black chenille stems (pipe cleaners)
Two 4 mm black half beads
2" magnetic tape
Tacky glue

Directions

1. Cut the following parts:

    Two black felt spiders (pattern piece #1)

    Eight black felt feet (pattern piece #2)

    Two lime green felt eyes (pattern piece #3)

    One orange felt nose (pattern piece #4)

    Two white felt fangs (pattern piece #5)

    Eight 3" pieces of black chenille stems

2. Bend the chenille stems as pictured to form spider legs.

3. Position and glue legs to one spider cut-out (#1) as shown. The legs may need to be trimmed so only $1/2$" of each leg is glued on the body.

4. Apply glue to the other spider cut-out. Matching the pair, glue the second body on top of the legs and the first body. Press the bodies together, especially in between the legs to secure.

5. Glue feet on the end of the legs as shown.

6. Position and glue the face on as shown. For the smile shape the wire first. Spread glue thinly on one side of the smile and then glue as shown to your magnet. Add spider fangs if you'd like.

7. Secure magnetic tape to back of spider.

#1

#2

#4

LEG

#3

#5

Wandering Spider Hat (K-6)

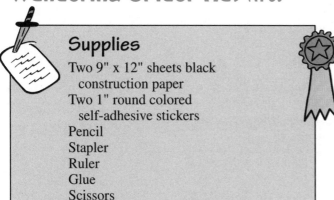

Supplies

Two 9" x 12" sheets black
   construction paper
Two 1" round colored
   self-adhesive stickers
Pencil
Stapler
Ruler
Glue
Scissors
Optional: Six tiny stickers

Wandering spiders live on the
ground. Most are extremely active.
Sounds like our kids, huh?

Directions

1. Glue two sheets of black construction paper together lengthwise and let them dry thoroughly.

2. Measuring up 3" from the bottom of the paper, use a pencil to draw a line running horizontally across the page. This is your starting line.

3. Measure 1$\frac{1}{2}$" in from the left side of the sheet and mark it.

4. Draw a line from that point to the top of the page.

5. Still moving towards the center of the sheet make another mark 1" to the right of your last line and draw a line from your starting point to the top. Continue on until you have eight lines.

6. Go to the right side and repeat this pattern. Do not forget to start 1 1/2" from the right side then make your markings 1" apart.

7. Cut out your spider hat to look like the following illustration. Be sure not to cut the spiders' legs off. Cut in between the legs.

8. For a quick finish, press 1" round colored self adhesive stickers in the center for eyes.

9. Fold the eight spider legs accordion style into $\frac{1}{2}$" sections. Experiment to see if you would like bigger or smaller bends.

10. Determine the hat size by measuring on the childs' head. Staple the two ends together. The spider legs should fold outward. A wandering spider has now been made.

117

Balloon Spider (K-6)

Supplies

Rubber cement
Two large oblong black balloons
Two tiny orange round balloons
Eight 12" long black chenille stem
    (pipe cleaners)

Directions

1. Blow up two of the black balloons.

2. Using rubber cement glue them together, tied end to end.

3. Glue two tiny orange balloons at the tip of one end of the black balloons. These are the spider eyes.

4. Attach black chenille sticks to make eight legs.

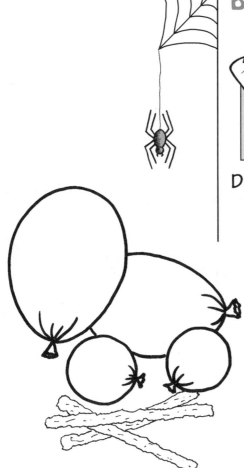

Spider Ring (K-6)

Supplies

Two black chenille stems (pipe cleaners)
$1/2$" to $3/4$" button with two holes
1" black pom-pom
Two 3 mm orange pom-poms
Tacky glue

Directions

1. Thread a chenille stem through a button.

2. Measure it around a finger and cut off the excess chenille stick.

3. Cut four 3" strips of chenille stem and glue them across the top of the button to form spider legs.

4. Glue a 1" diameter black pom-pom on top of the legs.

5. Glue two orange pom-poms on the black pom-pom for eyes.

6. Bend the spider legs once the glue is dry.

Spider Web Visor (K-6)

Supplies

Inexpensive white or orange visor
Black permanent ink marker
Plastic spider
Hot glue gun

Directions

1. Draw a spider web on the top of the visor with the marker.

2. Hot glue a plastic spider onto the web.

   Optional: Personalize the visor with the child's name.

Wiggly-Eyed Spider (K-6)

Supplies

Black styrofoam paint (found in
   craft stores)
One 2" x 4" styrofoam disc
Four 12" black chenille stems
   (pipe cleaners)
Two 15 mm moving eyes
Hot glue gun

Directions

1. Spray the styrofoam shape black.

2. Cut chenille stems in half and push into the styrofoam for legs.

3. Bend the ends of the legs in an upward loop.

4. Glue on moving eyes.

Supplies for Spider Favors

Spider Web Plaque (K-6)

Version #1
- 5" x 5" x $\frac{1}{2}$" thick wooden board
- Black spray paint
- Eight small nails
- Bright orange yarn
- Plastic spider
- Scissors
- Hammer

Version #2
- 4$\frac{1}{2}$" x 4$\frac{1}{2}$" black poster board
- Twelve to sixteen popsicle sticks
- Black spray paint
- Eight small nails
- Bright orange yarn
- Plastic spider
- Wood glue
- Scissors
- Hammer

Spider Magnet (K-6)

- 5" x 6" black felt
- 1" x 1" orange felt
- 2" x 2" white felt
- Three 12" black chenille stems (pipe cleaners)
- Two 4 mm black half beads
- 2" magnetic tape
- Tacky glue

Wandering Spider Hat (K-6)

- Two 9" x 12" sheets black construction paper
- Two 1" round colored self-adhesive stickers
- Pencil
- Stapler
- Ruler
- Glue
- Scissors
- Optional: Six tiny stickers

Balloon Spider (K-6)

- Rubber cement
- Two large oblong black balloons
- Two tiny orange round balloons
- Eight 12" long black chenille stem (pipe cleaners)

Spider Ring (K-6)

- Two black chenille stems (pipe cleaner)
- One $\frac{1}{2}$" to $\frac{3}{4}$" button with two holes
- 1" black pom-pom
- Two 3 mm orange pom-poms
- Tacky glue

Spider Web Visor (K-6)

- Inexpensive white or orange visor
- Black permanent ink marker
- Plastic spider
- Hot glue gun

Wiggly-Eyed Spider (K-6)

- Black styrofoam paint (found in craft stores)
- One 2" x 4" styrofoam disc
- Four 12" black chenille stems (pipe cleaners)
- Two 15 mm moving eyes
- Hot glue gun

Witch Favors

Witch Art (1-6)

Supplies

Plain white paper (one per child)
Pencil

Directions

1. On a sheet of plain paper very lightly draw the outline of the witch hat shown.

2. Tell the children to follow the outline of the witch hat continuously writing in a maze-like pattern. Use the word "witch".

3. Erase the pencil marks. Art has been created.

Witch Bags (K-6)

Supplies

Brown paper sack
Large witch stamp
Assorted treats
Paper hole puncher
Orange curling ribbon
Black curling ribbon
Scissors
Optional: Construction paper, yarn

Directions

1. Stamp a witch shape onto the lower half of the front of a paper lunch sack.

2. Put treats in the bags

3. Fold down the top of the bag once and punch two holes.

4. Thread and knot black and orange curling ribbon through the holes. Curl the ribbon.

   Optional: Make a witch on front of the bag using construction paper, yarn and glue.

121

Witch Bubbling Bath Brew (K-6)

Supplies

Small bottle of bubble bath
Paper
Markers
Glue

Directions

1. Soak the label off the bottle of bubble bath.

2. Make your own label —"Witch Bubbling Bath Brew"— and glue where the old label was.

Witch Magnet (K-6)

Supplies

9" x 6" black felt
$3^1/2$" x $3^1/2$" lime green felt
35" to 50" orange yarn
8 mm black moving eye
Black embroidery thread
Needle
Tacky glue
Scissors

Directions

1. Cut the following parts:

   One black felt witch head (pattern piece #1)

   One black felt hat brim (pattern piece #2)

   One black felt hat top (pattern piece #3)

   One black felt tooth (pattern piece #4)

   One lime green witch face (pattern piece #5)

2. Glue the witch's face onto her head.

3. Cut orange yarn into ten pieces, each $3^1/2$" long. Glue to the left side of the witch's head for hair.

4. Glue the hat over the hair. Then glue the brim over both the hair and the bottom of the hat.

5. Glue the eye on the face.

6. Using the embroidery thread make a french knot for a wart. Then, passing the thread back through the french knot, leave $1/2$" hanging loose (hair from the wart).

7. Glue the tooth into position.

122

#5

#4

#3

#1

#2

Witch Hat Treasure (K-6)

Supplies

Version #1
8" x 8" black poster board
   or
Paper cone cup
Trick-or-treat gift certificates
Candy
Tape, staple, or glue
Scissors
Optional: Glitter or star stickers, ribbon

Version #2
8" x 8" black poster board
2" styrofoam ball
Black craft hair
Two 8 mm moving eyes
One $1/4$" pom-pom (any color)
Trick-or-treat gift certificates
Candy
Tape, staple, or glue
Scissors
Optional: Glitter or star stickers, ribbon

Directions

Version #1

1. Trace and cut pattern piece #1 from poster board.

2. Make a cone shape out of the pattern. This will be the witch's hat. Tape, staple, or glue closed. (A paper cone cup may be substituted.)

3. Make the brim of the hat by tracing and cutting pattern piece #2 onto the remaining poster board.

4. Decorate the hat with glitter, stickers or a hat band. Use your imagination.

5. Place the cone shape on the hat brim.

6. Check out the grocery stores, restaurants, and bakeries in your area that offer trick-or-treat gift certificates. Hide a certificate and a piece of candy under the cone.

Version #2

1. Trace and cut pattern piece #1 from poster board.

2. Make a cone shape out of half the circle. Tape, staple or glue closed. This is the witch's dress.

3. With scissors, cut off part of the tip. Glue the styrofoam ball on the tip of the cone (this will be the witch's head).

4. Glue the hair, eyes, and pom-pom nose on the ball.

5. Trace hat pattern pieces #3 onto the poster board and cut out.

6. Make a cone for the hat (#3). Tape, staple or glue closed. Cut a circle slightly larger than the cone from poster board. This will be the brim. Glue hat to brim. Then glue hat to the styrofoam head.

7. Hide candy, trinkets or gift certificates under her dress.

   Optional: Decorate the witch's dress and hat with glitter, star stickers or ribbons.

#1

#3

#2

125

Witch On A Thimble (K-6)

Supplies

Wood thimble
Black paint
Tan craft foam
Make-up blush (any color)
5/8" round wood ball
Orange paint
Spanish moss
Broom bristles
2 inches of $1/8$" wooden dowel
Black poster board
9 inches of $1/8$" wide orange ribbon
Hot glue gun
Scissors

Directions

1. Paint the thimble black.

2. Cut legs (pattern piece #1) and arms (pattern piece #2) out of craft foam.

3. Paint two eyes on the wooden ball (witch head) with black paint. Use some of your own blush to give the cheeks color.

4. Paint the bottom rim of the thimble orange and paint on orange buttons.

5. Glue the wood ball (head) on top of the thimble using a hot glue gun.

6. Glue moss (hair) on top of the ball.

7. Tie the ribbon into a bow and glue at the neck.

8. Wrap and glue the arm around the body.

9. Cut bristles off a broom and hot glue onto the bottom of the dowel to look like a tiny witch's broom. Position the broom on the witch.

10. To make the witch's hat, cut two 1" diameter circles out of poster board. Make a cone shape out of one of the halves of circles. Tape, staple, or glue closed. Cut small slits at the bottom of the cone. Fold them (tabs) to the inside of the cone. Place glue on the tabs and press onto the other circle. Glue this hat to the wooden ball (head). For a final touch, glue a band of orange ribbon around the hat.

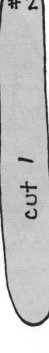

#2

cut 1

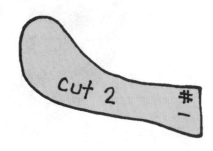

cut 2

#1

Supplies for Witch Favors

Witch Art (1-6)
Plain white paper (one per child)
Pencil

Witch Bags (K-6)
Brown paper sack
Large witch stamp
Assorted treats
Paper hole puncher
Orange curling ribbon
Black curling ribbon
Scissors
Optional: Construction paper, yarn

Witch Bubbling Bath Brew (K-6)
Small bottle of bubble bath
Paper
Markers
Glue

Witch Magnet (K-6)
9" x 6" black felt
3½" x 3½" lime green felt
35" to 50" orange yarn
8 mm black moving eye
Black embroidery thread
Needle
Tacky glue
Scissors

Witch's Hat Treasure (K-6)
Version #1
  8" x 8" black poster board
    or
  Paper cone cup

Trick-or-treat gift certificates
Candy
Tape, staple, or glue
Scissors
Optional: Glitter or star
  stickers, Ribbon
Version #2
  8" x 8" black poster board
  2" Styrofoam ball
  Black craft hair
  Two 8 mm moving eyes
  One ¼" pom-pom (any color)
  Trick-or-treat gift certificates
  Candy
  Tape, staple, or glue
  Scissors
  Optional: Glitter or star
    stickers, Ribbon

Witch On A Thimble (K-6)
Wood thimble
Black paint
Tan craft foam
Make-up blush (any color)
⅝" round wood ball
Orange paint
Spanish moss
Broom bristles
2 inches of ⅛" wooden dowel
Black poster board
9 inches of ⅛" wide orange ribbon
Hot glue gun
Scissors

Halloween School Parties:

The following 8 patterns may be used for Sand Art or Craft Foam Art.
Have fun! Be creative!

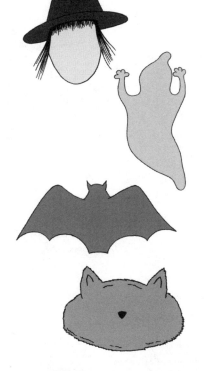

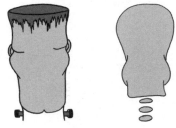

Extra Craft Ideas

These ideas can be adapted to fit any of the party themes.

Sand Art (K-6)

Supplies

White poster board
Outlines of Halloween shapes
Fine white sand (4 cups per batch)
Dry tempera paint (various colors,
  1$\frac{1}{2}$ tablespoons per batch)
School glue
Spoon
Water
Toothpick or bamboo skewer

Directions

1. Copy a Halloween pattern onto poster board. Great ideas for patterns can be found in coloring books, particularly preschool and kindergarten coloring books. You may also use the Halloween patterns located on the next three pages.

2. To make colored sand: Mix 1$\frac{1}{2}$ tablespoons of dry tempera paint to four cups of sand. Mix well. Add less or more paint to gain a lighter or darker shade.

3. To make the glue: Use equal parts of glue and water (one spoonful of school glue to one spoonful of water). Mix together and spread a thin layer on the Halloween picture.

4. Sprinkle colored sand onto the glued area. Shake excess off.

5. To use assorted colors of sand for the same picture, start with dark colors first then use lighter colors.

6. If necessary, use a pointed object to move the sand. A toothpick or bamboo skewer works well.

Craft Foam Art (K-6)

Supplies

Outlines of Halloween Shapes.
Craft foam (found at craft stores)
Scissors

Directions

1. Trace and cut Halloween shapes from craft foam.

2. Foam shapes can be used in the bathtub and will cling to tile bathtub walls.

129

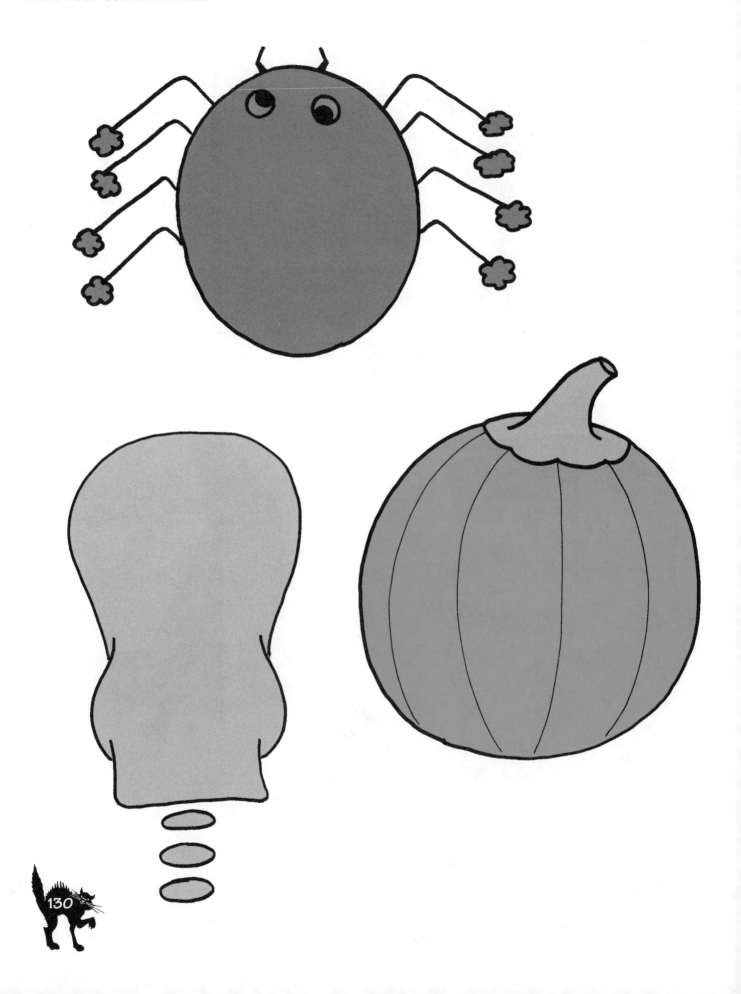

130

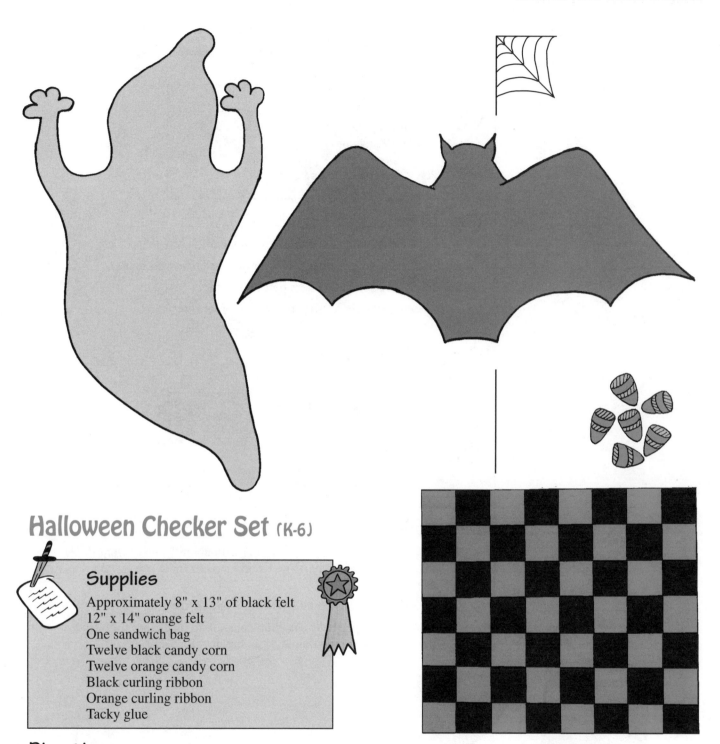

Halloween Checker Set (K-6)

Supplies

Approximately 8" x 13" of black felt
12" x 14" orange felt
One sandwich bag
Twelve black candy corn
Twelve orange candy corn
Black curling ribbon
Orange curling ribbon
Tacky glue

Directions

1. Cut 28 black squares $1^3/4$ x $1^3/4$ inches.

2. Glue the squares onto the orange felt in the same way a checker board is laid out. Make sure to spread glue evenly around all the edges of the black squares so they will lay flat.

3. For playing pieces use Halloween candy: Black candy corn for one side and orange for the other side. Put twelve pieces of each color in a clear sandwich bag. Tie with black and orange curling ribbon.

4. Roll up the checker board after it is completely dry and tie with black and orange curling ribbon. Attach the bag of candy with ribbon.

131

Halloween Pencil Toppers (K-6)

Supplies

Pencil
Modeling compound
Optional: Paints and/or markers,
   decorative items

Directions

1. Take compound and form it into any Halloween shape.
2. Stick it on the pencil and let it air dry hard (takes 24 hours).
3. Insert any decorative item before drying.

   Optional: Decorate with paints and/or markers.

Megan Lyons age 5
*"Smooshies are fun to play with.
I like them very much."*

Melissa Lyons age 8
*"Smooshies are fun and they
won't hurt you."*

Stephanie Lyons age 10
*"When you get mad, you can
punch a smooshie instead of
hitting a good pillow."*

Smooshies (K-6)

Supplies

One heavy balloon
Funnel
1 cup flour
Makes one smooshie.

Directions

1. Using the funnel, fill each balloon with about 1 cup of flour depending upon the size of the balloon. Gently tap the funnel as you fill it as full as possible.
2. Squeeze out as much air as possible and tie the end.

   Note: Do not use balloons which are sold in packages for birthday parties. They are too thin and can break.

Supplies for Extra Craft Ideas

Sand Art (K-6)

White poster board
Outlines of Halloween shapes
Fine white sand (4 cups per batch)
Dry tempera paint (various colors,
   1½ tablespoons per batch)
School glue
Spoon
Water
Toothpick or bamboo skewer

Craft Foam Art (K-6)

Outlines of Halloween shapes
Craft foam (found at craft stores.)
Scissors

Halloween Checker Set (K-6)

Approximately 8" x 13" of black felt
12" x 14" orange felt
One sandwich bag

Twelve black candy corn
Twelve orange candy corn
Black curling ribbon
Orange curling ribbon
Tacky glue

Halloween Pencil Toppers (K-6)

Pencil
Modeling compound
Optional: Paints and/or markers,
   decorative items

Smooshies (K-6)

One heavy balloon
Funnel
1 cup flour
Makes one smooshie.

CHAPTER FOUR
Treats

Helpful Hints for Refreshments

1. To make black frosting: First mix brown icing colors by Wilton® with chocolate frosting. Then add black icing colors by Wilton®, mixing until thoroughly blended.

2. Check with the teacher concerning any food allergies the students may have. If you want to make the peanut butter pumpkin recipe but there is a student who is allergic to peanuts, substitute the popcorn ghost recipe and shape into pumpkins not ghosts.

3. When decorating spider treats, spiders have eight legs.

4. Any treat that calls for ice cream or whipped topping is best to be made at school immediately before serving to avoid flops.

5. Candy Melts™ are made by Wilton® and can be found at stores that sell cake decorating items.

6. Skeleton toothpicks can be found at Halloween time. Look for them at discount stores.

7. Refreshments can be served from cardboard coffins, found at Halloween time. Look for them at discount stores.

8. Pumpkins carved out and cleaned can be used to hold dips or punch.

9. Canned frosting is used in all frosting recipes, but feel free to make your favorite homemade recipes if desired.

10. Grades 4-6 do fine serving themselves (buffet style). Other grades are usually to young. There can be exceptions, please ask the teacher, she knows her students.

Bat Treats

Chocolate Bat Cookies (K-6)

Ingredients and Supplies

One 9-ounce package of chocolate wafers
7 ounces of Wilton® Dark Cocoa Candy Melts™
Wax paper

Makes about 36 cookies.

Directions

1. Carefully cut the wafers into quarters. A serrated knife works best.
2. To make one bat lay two pieces of the cookie about 1/8 inch apart on waxed paper as in the drawing here.
3. Pour some melted candy melts at the middle of each bat to connect its wings and form a head.
4. Cool completely before lifting off the waxed paper.

Bat Cupcakes (K-6)

Ingredients

Cake mix (any flavor)
One 16-ounce canned chocolate frosting
Wilton® black icing colors
Wilton® brown icing colors
Two yellow or red M&Ms® (per cupcake)
Cupcake liners
Black construction paper

This recipe makes 24 - 28 cupcakes (²/3 full).

Directions

1. Bake cupcakes in cupcake liners that are all black or a Halloween pattern.
2. Make black frosting using the chocolate frosting and the black and brown icing colors (see details in Helpful Hints for Refreshments)
3. Frost the cupcakes.
4. Cut bat wings and ears out of black construction paper.
5. Slide the wings and ears into the cupcake.
6. Put M&Ms® eyes onto the cupcake.

Barbecued Bat Wings (K-6)

Ingredients

1/2 cup honey
1 cup soy sauce
1 cup water
Four garlic cloves (crushed)
Two dozen chicken wings
One 18-ounce barbecue sauce

This recipe makes 24 wings.

Directions

1. Mix the honey, soy sauce, water, and crushed garlic to make marinade.
2. In a covered dish, marinate the chicken wings overnight in the refrigerator.
3. Drain marinade, then broil wings for 8 minutes on each side.
4. Serve with barbecue sauce.

Bat Cake (K-6)

Ingredients and Supplies

Cake mix (any flavor)
One package black string licorice
One 16-ounce canned chocolate frosting
Wilton® black icing color
Wilton® brown icing color
One 12-ounce canned white frosting
One Hostess® Ding Dong™ or chocolate creme-
   filled cupcake
Two cinnamon imperials
3" x 3" black construction paper

Serves one class if pieces are small.

Directions

1. Bake the cake in a round cake pan.
2. Cut the cake in half and position it on your serving board as in the drawing.
3. With black string licorice, outline the cake to form a wing pattern.
4. Mix chocolate frosting and the brown and black icing colors (as described in Helpful Hints for Refreshments) to make black icing for frosting the cake.
5. Use the black frosting to fill in the areas inside the licorice lines.
6. Frost the sides of your cake and the leftover top area with white frosting.
7. Place the Hostess® Ding Dong™ or cupcake on top of the cake

where the wings meet.

8. Frost the Ding Dong™ with black frosting to match the cake.

9. Place cinnamon imperials on the Ding Dong™ for eyes.

10. Cut ears out of black construction paper and insert into the cake as in the drawing.

    Optional: If you have taken cake decorating lessons and feel creative, use a star tip #16 to do the fill ins and a #233 tip for the bat's face.

Bat Cookies (K-6)

Ingredients and Supplies

$1/2$ cup shortening
$1/4$ cup butter
Two eggs
1 teaspoon vanilla
1 cup sugar
$2 1/2$ cups all purpose flour
$1/4$ teaspoon salt
1 teaspoon baking powder
One 16-ounce canned chocolate frosting
Wilton® black icing colors
Wilton® brown icing colors
Cinnamon imperials
Bat cookie cutter

This recipe makes 15 large cookies or 24 smaller cookies.

Directions

1. Mix the shortening, butter, eggs, vanilla and sugar together.

2. Sift the flour, salt, and baking powder together.

3. Mix the flour mixture into the shortening mixture.

4. Refrigerate dough for one hour, then roll out into $1/8$ inch thickness.

5. Cut with your favorite bat cookie cutter. Bake at 400° F for 6-8 minutes on ungreased cookie sheet.

6. Mix chocolate frosting and the brown and black icing colors (as described in Helpful Hints for Refreshments) to make black icing for frosting the cookies.

7. Add two cinnamon imperials for the bat's eyes.

Ingredients for Bat Treats

Chocolate Bat Cookies (K-6)

One 9-ounce package of
  chocolate wafers
7 ounces of Wilton® Dark Cocoa
  Candy Melts™
Wax paper
Makes about 36 cookies.

Bat Cupcakes (K-6)

Cake mix (any flavor)
One 16-ounce canned chocolate
  frosting
Wilton® black icing colors
Wilton® brown icing colors
Two yellow or red M&Ms®
  (per cupcake)
Cupcake liners
Black construction paper
This recipe makes 24 - 28 cupcakes
  (2/3 full).

Barbecued Bat Wings (K-6)

1/2 cup honey
1 cup soy sauce
1 cup water
Four garlic cloves (crushed)
Two dozen chicken wings
One 18-ounce barbecue sauce
This recipe makes 24 wings.

Bat Cake (K-6)

Cake mix (any flavor)
One package black string licorice
One 16-ounce canned chocolate
  frosting

Wilton® black icing color
Wilton® brown icing color
One 12-ounce canned white frosting
One Hostess® Ding Dong™ or
  chocolate creme-filled cupcake
Two cinnamon imperials
3" x 3" black construction paper
Serves one class if pieces are small.

Bat Cookies (K-6)

1/2 cup shortening
1/4 cup butter
Two eggs
1 teaspoon vanilla
1 cup sugar
2 1/2 cups all purpose flour
1/4 teaspoon salt
1 teaspoon baking powder
One 16-ounce canned chocolate
  frosting
Wilton® black icing colors
Wilton® brown icing colors
Cinnamon imperials
Bat cookie cutter
This recipe makes 15 large cookies
  or 24 smaller cookies.

Cat Treats

Meow Meow Cookies (K-6)

Ingredients

$3/4$ cup shortening
Two eggs
1 teaspoon vanilla
1 cup sugar
$2^1/2$ cups all purpose flour
$1/4$ teaspoon salt
1 teaspoon baking powder
Thirty pecan halves
Thirty M&Ms®
Forty-five pretzel sticks cut in half
Optional: Use refrigerator case sugar cookie dough.

This recipe makes 15 large cookies or 24 smaller cookies.

Directions

1. Mix the shortening, eggs, and vanilla together.
2. Sift the flour, salt, and baking powder together.
3. Mix the flour mixture into the shortening mixture.
4. Refrigerate dough for one hour, then form your cookie dough into a thick tube shape.
5. Slice cookies from this roll, cutting each about $1/4$ inch thick.
6. Press two pecan halves on the top of each cookie for the cat's ears.
7. Use two M&Ms® for the cat's eyes.
8. Cut pretzel sticks in half. Press in three halves on each side for whiskers.
9. Bake at 400° F for 6-8 minutes on ungreased cookie sheet.
10. Cool the cookies before removing them from the cookie sheet.

Fishy Cat Snacks (K-6)

Ingredients

1 cup M&Ms®
$1/2$ cup raisins
$1/2$ cup nuts
3 cups fish crackers
1 cup pretzels

Makes six 1-cup servings.

Directions

1. Combine all of the ingredients to form a snack mix.
2. Divide the mix into 1-cup servings.

141

Cool Black Cats (K-6)

Ingredients

One large scoop of chocolate ice cream
1/4 cup chocolate syrup
15 inches of black licorice strings (cut into six
  2 1/2-inch pieces)
One 4-inch black licorice string
Two candy corns
Three M&Ms®

Multiply these ingredients by the number to be served.

Directions

1. Put a large scoop of ice cream in a dish, then pour chocolate syrup on top. This is the cat's "face."

2. Decorate the face using candy corn for the ears, M&Ms® for the eyes and nose, and the short licorice strings for the whiskers. Use the long licorice string for the tail.

Cat Open-Face Sandwiches (K-6)

Ingredients

Bread
Round lunch meat
Thin slices of a round vegetable (such as cucumbers,
  carrots, cherry tomatoes, and zucchini)
Chocolate chips
Celery or carrot sticks
Black olives
Green or red pepper

Directions

1. Lay the lunch meat on a piece of bread.

2. The thin slices of a round vegetable becomes the eyes. Add chocolate chips for the pupils.

3. Slice the carrot or celery very thin to become whiskers.

4. Cut ears out of the lunch meat and overlap them on the face.

5. Use a circular slice of black olive for the nose.

6. Place a thin, curved slice of green or red pepper on the sandwich as a mouth.

Cats on a Fence Cake (K-6)

Ingredients

Cake mix (any flavor)
One 12-ounce canned white frosting
Six to eight pretzel rods
Four 1-inch round cookies
Candy corns
24 inches of black licorice strings

Makes a 13" x 9" cake.

Directions:

1. Bake a 13" x 9" cake.
2. Ice with white frosting.
3. Use pretzel rods to make a fence.
4. Make two cats sitting on the fence. Use two cookies to form each cat's body.
5. Add candy corn for their ears.
6. Use black string licorice (cut into 1 1/2 inch pieces) for the whiskers.
7. Tuck a 3-inch piece of licorice under each cat's bottom for a tail.

Garfield Cupcakes (K-6)

Ingredients and Supplies

Cake mix (any flavor)
Cupcake liners
One 16-ounce canned orange frosting
Wilton® White Candy Melts™
Pink jelly beans
Potato chips
Yellow fruit roll-ups
Orange chenille stems (pipe cleaners)
Optional: Garfield Wilton® Candy Molds

This recipe makes 24 -28 cupcakes (2/3 full).

Directions

1. Ice the cupcakes with the orange frosting.
2. Use two white round candy melts for Garfield's eyes and a pink jelly bean placed lengthwise horizontally for his nose.
3. Use two curved potato chips for his ears. Poke these into the frosting.
4. Place a yellow fruit roll-up strip around his nose to make a funny mouth.
5. Bend the chenille stem in half and twist. This will be his tail.

   Optional: You may also make Garfield candy and place onto an iced cupcake. To make the candy use a Wilton® Garfield candy mold, and Wilton® Candy Melts™.

What makes a school Halloween party fun?

Mark Ripple, 13 years old:
"Garfield - he's also fun to read and watch."

Jonathan Krohn, 9 years old:
"Food - pop and cupcakes."

Garfield Characters: © 1978
United Feature Syndicate, Inc.

143

Ingredients for Cat Treats

Meow Meow Cookies (K-6)

3/4 cup shortening
Two eggs
1 teaspoon vanilla
1 cup sugar
2 1/2 cups all purpose flour
1/4 teaspoon salt
1 teaspoon baking powder
Thirty pecan halves
Thirty M&Ms®
Forty-five pretzel sticks cut in half
Optional: Use refrigerator case
   sugar cookie dough.
This recipe makes 15 large cookies
   or 24 smaller cookies.

Fishy Cat Snacks (K-6)

1 cup M&Ms®
1/2 cup raisins
1/2 cup nuts
3 cups fish crackers
1 cup pretzels
Makes six 1-cup servings.

Cool Black Cats (K-6)

One large scoop of chocolate ice
   cream
1/4 cup chocolate syrup
15 inches of black licorice strings
   (cut into six 2 1/2-inch pieces)
One 4-inch black licorice string
Two candy corn
Three M&Ms®
Multiply these ingredients by the
   number to be served.

Cat Open-Face Sandwiches (K-6)

Bread
Round lunch meat
Thin slices of a round vegetable
   (such as cucumbers, carrots,
   cherry tomatoes, and zucchini)
Chocolate chips
Celery or carrot sticks
Black olives
Green or red pepper

Cats on a Fence Cake (K-6)

Cake mix (any flavor)
One 12-ounce canned white frosting
Six to eight Pretzel rods
Four 1-inch round cookies
Candy corns
24 inches of black licorice strings
Makes a 13" x 9" cake.

Garfield Cupcakes (K-6)

Cake mix (any flavor)
Cupcake liners
One 16-ounce canned orange frosting
Wilton® White Candy Melts™
Pink jelly beans
Potato chips
Yellow fruit roll-ups
Orange chenille stems (pipe cleaners)
Optional: Garfield Wilton®
   Candy Molds
This recipe makes 24-28 cupcakes
   (2/3 full).
Garfield Characters:© 1978 United
   Feature Syndicate, Inc.

Frankenstein Treats

Frank-en-steins (K-6)

Ingredients and Supplies

Mini cocktail frankfurters (about six per child)
Mustard
Ketchup
Pickles
Toothpicks
Steins (cups)

Directions

1. Cook the frankfurters in a crock pot at school. Follow crock pot directions for cooking.

2. Stick on toothpicks and place in "steins" (a "stein" is a German mug or cup; hence the name "Frank-en-steins"). Give a few franks to each child.

3. Allow the kids to garnish their franks with the condiments.

Frankensteins Eyeball Unbaked Cookies (K-6)

Ingredients and Supplies

$1/2$ cup butter
$1^1/2$ cups peanut butter
$2^1/2$ cups powdered sugar
1 teaspoon vanilla
Wilton® White Candy Melts™
Wax paper

Makes 2 dozen cookies.

Directions

1. Cream the butter and peanut butter, then add the powdered sugar and vanilla. Blend well.

2. Form this mixture into 1-inch diameter balls.

3. Place these "eyeballs" on waxed paper and refrigerate for one hour.

4. Follow the directions on the package for melting the candies.

5. Take a few of the cookies out of the refrigerator at a time. Then, one cookie at a time poke a toothpick into the cookie and dip the cookie into the melted candy. Immerse the cookie almost all the way into the melt, leaving a small portion at the top not dipped. This will leave a circle to form an eyeball look.

6. Lay the "eyeballs" on wax paper until hardened.

 145

Cheesy Frankenstein "Sculpture" (K-6)

Ingredients

Square crackers
Soft cheese spread (any flavor)
Stalk of celery
Two green olives

One Frankenstein feeds the whole class.

Directions:

1. Spread the cheese on the crackers. Lay them flat on a cookie tray lengthwise and stack them until you have a pile about 6 inches long, all glued by cheese.

2. Cut a piece of celery approximately 3-4 inches from the leafy end of the stalk. This will be Frankenstein's head.

3. Using the cheese spread, attach the head to the crackers (the body).

4. Cut the remainder of the celery into five pieces, two (at the leafy ends) about 5 inches long to form arms, two about 4 inches long for the legs, and a 2-inch chunk for the neck bolts.

5. Using cheese spread, attach the arms to the body.

6. Attach the legs to the body with cheese spread.

7. Slice the 2-inch chunk in half, and use these pieces for the bolts coming out of Frankenstein's neck. Attach them with the cheese spread.

8. Attach two green olives to the head for eyes, using the cheese.

Frankensteins' Deviled "Eyes" (K-6)

Ingredients and Supplies

Six hard-boiled eggs
1/4 teaspoon salt
1/2 teaspoon prepared mustard
1/8 teaspoon pepper
3-4 tablespoons mayonnaise

Four black or green olives
Wilton® Red Icing Color
Thin paint brush (new)
Green paper plates

This recipe makes 6 pairs of eyes.

Directions

1. When the hard-boiled eggs have cooled, cut them in half.

2. Remove the yolks and set aside the whites. Mix the yokes with the salt, mustard, pepper, and mayonnaise until creamy.

3. Spoon the yolk mixture back into the whites, placing two eggs on each paper plate.

4. Slice the olives about 1/8 inch thick. Place a slice in the middle of each egg to represent the center of the eye.

5. Mix a dab of red icing color with a drop of water. Then dip a thin paintbrush into the red food coloring and draw blood vessels, connecting the olives to the egg whites.

Frankenstein Caramel Apples (K-6)

Ingredients and Supplies

One 14-ounce package of caramels
1 cup mini marshmallows
Five to six apples
Five to six popsicle sticks

For each caramel apple you will need:

1 tablespoon orange sprinkles
Two green jelly beans
4 inches of red string licorice
2 inches of black string licorice
Two green gumdrops

This recipe makes 5 - 6 candy apples.

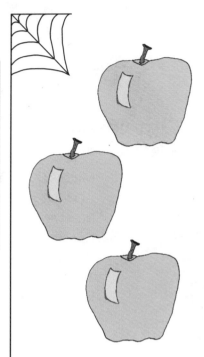

Directions

1. Wash the apples and let them dry.

2. Over medium heat, melt the caramels and marshmallows in a sauce pan. Add one tablespoon or more of water if needed to thin the mixture.

3. Insert a popsicle stick into the stem end of each apple. Dip the apple into the caramel mixture. Lay the apple on wax paper that has been sprinkled with powdered sugar.

4. Working quickly, apply the orange sprinkles for Frankenstein's hair.

5. Add two green jelly beans—turned lengthwise horizontally—for his eyes.

6. Slice a 1-inch piece of red licorice string for the mouth.

7. Use the reminder of red licorice to make a scar.

8. Push two gumdrops into Frankenstein's neck for bolts.

9. Cut the black licorice into $1/4$-inch pieces. Use three over each eye for eyelashes.

Frankenstein's Eyeball Fruit Salad (K-6)

Ingredients and Supplies

4 cups Honeydew melon (approximately one melon)
4 cups Cantaloupe melon (approximately one melon)
$3^1/2$ cups red grapes
$3^1/2$ cups green grapes
30 bamboo skewers
Approximately $1/2$ cup of fruit is needed per skewer.

This recipe makes 30 servings.

Directions

1. With the small size of a melon-baller, make eyeball shaped pieces of honeydew and cantaloupe. Mix the melon in a bowl.

2. Mix in the red and green grapes.

3. Serve in a small bowl with a bamboo skewer. The kids put the fruit onto the skewer.

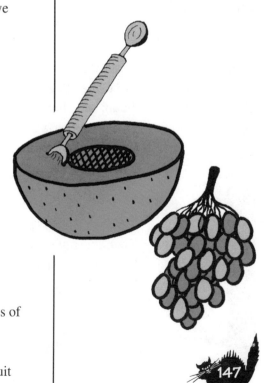

Ingredients for Frankenstein Treats

Frank-en-steins (K-6)

Mini cocktail frankfurters
  (about six per child)
Mustard
Ketchup
Pickles
Toothpicks
Steins (cups)

Frankensteins Eyeball Unbaked Cookies (K-6)

1/2 cup butter
1 1/2 cups peanut butter
2 1/2 cups powdered sugar
1 teaspoon vanilla
Wilton® White Candy Melts™
Wax paper
Makes 2 dozen cookies.

Cheesy Frankenstein "Sculpture" (K-6)

Square crackers
Soft cheese spread (any flavor)
Stalk of celery
Two green olives
One Frankenstein feeds the
  whole class.

Frankensteins' Deviled "Eyes" (K-6)

Six hard-boiled eggs
1/4 teaspoon salt
1/2 teaspoon prepared mustard
1/8 teaspoon pepper
3-4 tablespoons mayonnaise
Four black or green olives

Wilton® Red Icing Color
Thin paint brush (new)
Green paper plates
This recipe makes 6 pairs of eyes.

Frankenstein Caramel Apple (K-6)

One 14-ounce package of caramels
1 cup mini marshmallows
Five to six apples
Five to six popsicle sticks

For each caramel apple
  you will need:
1 tablespoon orange sprinkles
Two green jelly beans
4 inches of red string licorice
2 inches of black string licorice
Two green gumdrops
This recipe makes 5-6 candy apples.

Frankenstein's Eyeball Fruit Salad (K-6)

4 cups Honeydew melon (approximately one melon)
4 cups Cantaloupe melon
  (approximately one melon)
3 1/2 cups red grapes
3 1/2 cups green grapes
30 bamboo skewers
Approximately 1/2 cup of fruit is
  needed per skewer.
This recipe makes 30 servings.

Ghost Treats

Chilling Ghost Ice Cream (K-6)

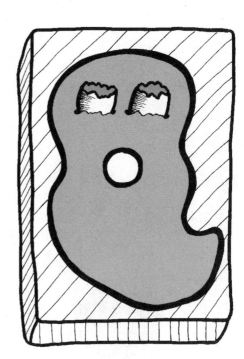

Ingredients

Two gallons of vanilla ice cream
Two cans of whipped cream
Sixty-four M&Ms®

This recipe serves 32 1-cup servings.

Directions

1. Scoop out one cup of softened vanilla ice cream.

2. When you put it in the bowl, shake the ice cream off the spoon so it creates an irregular ghost shape.

3. Squirt whipped cream on or around the ghost.

4. For eyes, use two M&M's®.

5. Serve immediately.

Flaming Ghost (K-6)

Ingredients and Supplies

Cake mix (any flavor)
One 16-ounce canned white frosting
One package of black string licorice
One egg
Lemon extract
Matches
Two sugar cubes

Makes a 9" x 13" cake.

Directions

1. Bake the cake in a 9" x 13" pan.

2. Ice with white frosting.

3. Outline a ghost shape on top of the cake with black string licorice.

4. Crack an egg in half, discarding the egg or setting it aside in the refrigerator for later use.

5. Rinse out the eggshell halves and let them dry.

6. Position the eggshell halves onto the cake (broken ends up) for the ghost's eyes.

7. Soak two sugar cubes in lemon extract. Put one inside each shell.

8. Turn off the lights and shut the shades.

9. Light the sugar cubes. Pay attention and watch your flaming ghost, the sugar cubes will dissolve quickly and the flame will disappear.

149

Popcorn Ghosts (K-6)

Ingredients and Supplies

4 ounces butter or margarine (one stick)
$1/2$ cup light corn syrup
1 cup sugar
1 teaspoon baking soda
13 cups popped popcorn
Twelve popsicle sticks
Twenty-four jelly beans

Makes 12 ghosts

Directions

1. Mix the butter, corn syrup, and sugar in a saucepan, bringing the mixture to a boil. Let it boil for about 3 minutes.

2. Add the baking soda and stir. Mixture will get foamy.

3. Mix immediately with the popcorn.

4. Shape the popcorn mixture into ghost shapes quickly.

5. Quickly stick a popsicle stick into the bottom of each ghost.

6. Stick two jelly beans on for eyes.

   Tip: Spread softened butter on your hands first to keep the popcorn from sticking to them.

Nutter Butter® Ghost (K-6)

Ingredients

6 ounces vanilla flavored almond bark
One package Nutter Butter® Cookies
Small bag mini chocolate chips

This recipe makes about 32 cookies.

Directions

1. Follow the instructions on the package of almond bark and melt the bark in a saucepan.

2. Briefly immerse two-thirds of each cookie into the melted bark.

3. Hold each cookie above the saucepan until the cookie stops dripping.

4. Lay the cookies on a wire rack, immediately placing two chocolate chips on each for eyes.

5. Cool completely.

Easy Haunted House Cake (K-6)

Ingredients and Supplies

Two frozen pound cakes
One 16-ounce canned chocolate frosting
Brown cardboard (roof and tombstones)
Pretzel sticks
Eight marshmallows
Clean dry tree twigs
Brown sugar
Decorating icing (various colors)
Decorating bag
Decorating tip #4
Optional: 1/2 cup white frosting

One haunted house feeds the whole class

Directions

1. Frost a pound cake with chocolate frosting, then stack the second cake on top and frost it. Place it on a serving platter.

2. Slit a piece of cardboard lengthwise. Fold it in half to form a peaked roof. Place it on top of the cake and ice with chocolate frosting.

3. Cut tombstone shapes from cardboard and place them around the house securing them with frosting.

4. Place clean dry tree twigs around the house, also securing them with frosting.

5. Build a fence with pretzels sticks and marshmallows and secure it with frosting.

6. Fill your decorating bag with frosting and pipe windows and a door onto the haunted house.

7. Make a pathway up to the door by using a small amount of frosting to create the path's shape and sprinkling this with brown sugar.

   Optional: Using white frosting, pipe a skeleton leaning on a tombstone. (Use the directions from the skeleton cupcakes page 158)

Ghost Cupcakes (K-6)

Ingredients

Cake mix (any flavor)
Cupcake liners
Frozen whipped topping
Small bag of mini chocolate chips

This recipe make 24-28 cupcakes (2/3 full).

Directions

1. Using the directions on the box, bake cupcakes, let cool.

2. Spoon a blob of thawed whipped topping on top of the cupcake in the shape of a ghost.

3. Use mini chocolate chips for eyes. Serve immediately.

151

Ingredients for Ghost Treats

Chilling Ghost Ice Cream (K-6)

Two gallons of vanilla ice cream
Two cans of whipped cream
Sixty-four M&Ms®
This recipe serves 32 1-cup
   servings.

Flaming Ghosts (K-6)

Cake mix (any flavor)
One 16-ounce canned white frosting
One package of black string licorice
One egg
Lemon extract
Matches
Two sugar cubes
Makes a 9" x 13" cake

Popcorn Ghosts (K-6)

4 ounces butter or margarine
   (one stick)
1/2 cup light corn syrup
1 cup sugar
1 teaspoon baking soda
13 cups popped popcorn
Twelve popsicle sticks
Twenty-four jelly beans
Makes 12 ghosts.

Nutter Butter Ghost (K-6)

6 ounces vanilla flavored
   almond bark
One package Nutter
   Butter® Cookies
Small bag mini chocolate chips
This recipe makes about 32 cookies.

Easy Haunted House Cake (K-6)

Two frozen pound cakes
One 16-ounce canned
   chocolate frosting
Brown cardboard (roof and
   tombstones)
Pretzel sticks
Eight marshmallows
Clean dry tree twigs
Brown sugar
Decorating icing (various colors)
Decorating bag
Decorating tip #4
Optional: 1/2 cup white frosting
One haunted house feeds the
   whole class

Ghost Cupcakes (K-6)

Cake mix (any flavor)
Cupcake liners
Frozen whipped topping
Small bag of mini chocolate chips
This recipe make 24-28 cupcakes
   (2/3 full).

Pumpkin Treats

Jack-O-Lantern Ice Cream (K-6)

Ingredients and Supplies

Oranges (one per child)
One gallon ice cream or sherbet (any flavor)
Thirty-two green gumdrops
Option A: Assorted fruit, cut-up (16 cups)
Option B: Black permanent marker

This amount of ice cream or fruit yields 32 servings of $1/2$ cup each.

Directions

1. Buy the largest oranges you can find. Make sure they are flat on the bottom so they can stand up without rolling.

2. Slice off the top of the orange as if you were carving a pumpkin. Set it aside as a lid.

3. Carve out the orange without tearing the orange rind.

4. Cut a face pattern into the remainder of the orange rind..

5. Fill the orange with $1/2$ cup of ice cream.

6. Cut a hole in the top of the lid, then place the lid back onto the filled orange. Place a green gumdrop in the hole on top to anchor the lid and represent a stem.

8. Freeze the filled oranges. Serve immediately after removing from freezer.

   Option A: Fill the orange with fruit salad.

   Option B: Using a permanent marker, draw a pumpkin face on the orange instead of carving one.

Easy Pumpkin Cookies (K-6)

Ingredients

Two round, flat store-bought cookies
1 tablespoon of canned chocolate frosting per child
One green gumdrop per cookie

Multiply these ingredients by the number to be served.

Directions

1. Spread frosting on the flat side of one cookie.

2. Attach the second cookie on top of the first one.

3. Attach a green gumdrop in the center of the cookie with a dab of frosting.

153

Pumpkin Fruit Spears (K-6)

Ingredients and Supplies

Assorted fruit
Bamboo skewers (1 per child)
One large pumpkin

Use approximately 1/4 cup of fruit per skewer.

Directions

1. Cut assorted fruit into 1-inch cubes and slide onto bamboo skewers, leaving about 3 inches open at one end. Apples and bananas will brown so avoid using them or cut and attach them right before you are ready to serve.

2. When you are ready to serve the fruit, stick 3 inches of each skewer into the pumpkin, arranging the skewers evenly around the pumpkin. Let the children help themselves to a skewer.

   Note: This makes a nice centerpiece.

Peanut Butter Pumpkins (K-6)

Ingredients and Supplies

16 cups popped popcorn.
1 1/2 cups sugar
1 1/2 cups corn syrup
1/2 cup peanut butter.
3/4 teaspoon vanilla.
Clear plastic wrap
Green ribbon or yarn
Black construction paper
School glue

This recipe makes 16 pumpkins.

Directions

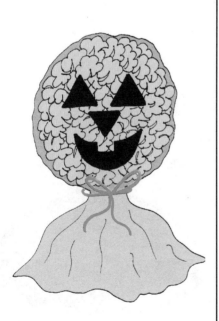

1. Mix the sugar and corn syrup in a saucepan, bringing the mixture to a boil over medium heat.

2. Remove the pan from the heat and stir in the peanut butter and vanilla.

3. Mix immediately with the popped popcorn. Butter your hands before forming the popcorn mixture into sixteen rounded balls.

4. Wrap each ball in clear plastic wrap, tying the top together with green ribbon or yarn.

5. Glue on jack-o-lantern facial features cut from black construction paper.

Apple Peanut Butter Raisin Pumpkins (K-6)

Ingredients

Apple ($^{1}/2$ per child)
Creamy peanut butter
Sixteen raisins
Two green gumdrops

Optional: Cheese Spread

This recipe makes 2 pumpkins.

Directions

1. Cut each apple in half, removing any seeds.

2. Spread peanut butter across each half.

3. Let the kids decorate their pumpkin faces using raisins for the eyes, nose, and mouth. Have them add a green gumdrop as a stem.

   Optional: Try cheese spread if you would like the pumpkin faces to be orange.

Pumpkin Donut Dessert (K-6)

Ingredients

One chocolate donut
   per child
$^{1}/2$ cup orange sherbet
One green gumdrop (stem)

One piece candy corn (nose)
Two M&Ms® (eyes)
Small candies

This recipe makes 1 dessert.

Directions

1. Fill the hole of the donut with a scoop of sherbet.

2. Let the kids decorate their pumpkin faces with the remaining ingredients as suggested above.

Healthy Pumpkin (K-6)

Ingredients and Supplies

Orange or apple (one per child)
Orange crepe paper
Green ribbon or yarn (6 inches per child)
Black felt
School glue

This recipe makes 1 pumpkin.

Directions

1. Using orange crepe paper wrap up an orange or apple.

2. Tie the paper closed with green ribbon or yarn.

3. Using black felt, cut out a pumpkin face and glue it on.

Ingredients for Pumpkin Treats

Jack- O- Lantern Ice cream (K-6)

Oranges (one per child)
One gallon ice cream or sherbet (any flavor)
Thirty-two green gumdrops
Option A: Assorted fruit, cut-up (16 cups)
Option B: Black permanent marker
This amount of ice cream or fruit yields 32 servings of 1/2 cup each.

Easy Pumpkin Cookies (K-6)

Two round, flat store-bought cookies
1 tablespoon of canned chocolate frosting per child
One green gumdrop per cookie
Multiply these ingredients by the number to be served.

Pumpkin Fruit Spears (K-6)

Assorted fruit
Bamboo skewers (1 per child)
One large pumpkin
Use approximately 1/4 cup of fruit per skewer.

Peanut Butter Pumpkins (K-6)

16 cups popped popcorn.
1 1/2 cups sugar
1 1/2 cups corn syrup
1/2 cup peanut butter.

3/4 teaspoon vanilla.
Clear plastic wrap
Green ribbon or yarn
Black construction paper
School Glue
This recipe makes 16 pumpkins.

Apple Peanut Butter Raisin Pumpkins (K-6)

Apple (1/2 per child)
Creamy peanut butter
Sixteen raisins
Two green gumdrops
Optional: Cheese spread
This recipe makes 2 pumpkins.

Pumpkin Donut Dessert (K-6)

One chocolate donut per child
1/2 cup orange sherbet
One green gumdrop (stem)
One piece candy corn (nose)
Two M&Ms® (eyes)
This recipe makes 1 dessert.

Healthy Pumpkin (K-6)

Orange or apple (one per child)
Orange crepe paper
Green ribbon or yarn (6 inches per child)
Black felt
School glue
This recipe makes 1 pumpkin.

Skeleton Treats

Creamy Tombstone Dessert (K-6)

Ingredients

4 ounces butter or margarine (one stick)
2 1/4 cups cookie crumbs
1/2 cup sugar
One 8-ounce package of cream cheese, softened
One 12-ounce whipped topping, thawed
2 1/2 cups water
One package (8 serving size) gelatin dessert
Rectangular shaped sandwich cookies
Decorating icing (various colors)
Decorating bag
Decorating tip #2
Candy corns
Candy pumpkins

This recipe makes 15 servings.

1. Melt the margarine. Add 2 cups of cookie crumbs and 1/4 cup of the sugar to the margarine. Mix well. Press the crumb mixture into the bottom of a 13" x 9" pan.

2. Blend the other 1/4 cup of sugar with the cream cheese.

3. Gently fold 6 ounces (3/4 cup) of the whipped topping into the cream cheese mixture. Spread this topping over the cookie crumb mixture.

4. Boil water. Add the gelatin dessert, stirring until dissolved (about three minutes).

5. In a (2 cup) measuring cup put 1/2 cup cold water and add ice cubes until you get to the 1 1/2 cup marking. Stir this mixture into the dissolved gelatin dessert until the gelatin starts to get thick. Then spoon out any extra ice cubes pieces.

6. Poor the gelatin mixture into the pan on top of the cream cheese.

7. Store in the refrigerator until firm (approximately 3 hours).

8. After refrigerating, spread the remaining whipped topping on top of the dessert, then sprinkle with remaining cookie crumbs.

9. The next step is to decorate the cookies that will be added to the cake. Decorate the cookies with skulls and crossbones. Do not decorate the bottom 1/3 of the cookie. Push the undecorated side of the cookie into the dessert in rows. Do this prior to serving because the cookies will get mushy if they are in the cake too long.

10. Sprinkle candy corn and tiny candy pumpkins on top of the cake in between the tombstone.

Skeleton Cupcakes (K-6)

Ingredients and Supplies

Cake mix (any flavor)
One 16-ounce canned white frosting
One 16-ounce canned chocolate frosting
Grey poster board
Black permanent marker
Decorating bag
Decorating tip #4

Makes approximately 24-28 cupcakes.

Directions

1. Bake the cupcakes following the directions on the box of cake mix.

2. Frost them with chocolate frosting.

3. Cut out a tombstone shape (about 3" tall x 2" wide) out of the poster board. With the marker, write R.I.P. on the tombstone. Insert a tombstone in the icing of each cupcake.

4. Using a cake decorating bag with a #4 tip, pipe a skeleton on the tombstone with white frosting. Here's how: Squeeze out a $1/2$-inch ball near the top of the tombstone. This will be the top part of the skull. Below that squeeze out a smaller dab for the jaw. Now, to form the spine pipe out about five connected dots, beginning at the jaw. Next squeeze out enough frosting to pipe the shoulder blades and arms. Make the ribs by piping figure eights across the spine. Add hip bones below the rib cage, connecting leg bones to the hips and feet bones to the legs. (Add a small dot at each elbow and hip joint.) Finally, add toes and fingers.

Karen Simpson:

"You can buy cupcakes all ready made and iced. Then all you have to do is make white icing and pipe on the skeleton. Its easy!"

Skeleton Cookies (K-6)

Ingredients and Supplies

Four large egg whites
$1^3/4$ cups sugar
$1/2$ teaspoon grated
   orange peel
$1/2$ teaspoon baking powder

$1^1/2$ cups finely chopped, salted, roasted almond
$1^3/4$ cups flour
Plastic wrap
Bakers Joy®

This recipe makes about 30 cookies.

Directions:

1. Put the egg whites, sugar, orange peel and baking powder in a mixing bowl and beat with an electric mixer on medium speed.

2. Add the nuts and flour slowly, beating at medium speed until the mixture is creamy and thoroughly blended.

3. Cover the bowl with plastic wrap and chill the dough for one hour or more.

4. Form the dough into round golf-ball size pieces. Working on a floured area with slightly floured hands roll a ball into a six-inch rope.

5. Cut the rope in half and roll each piece again into a 6-inch rope.

6. With each 6-inch piece, turn up about one inch of dough on each end. Pinch this folded section to make a bone shape.

7 Repeat the above steps until all the dough is gone.

8. Spray Baker's Joy® onto the cookie sheet.

9. Lay the bones on the sheet leaving an inch or so between. Bake at 325° F until lightly brown for about 15-20 minutes.

10. Remove from the cookie sheet and lay on a wire rack to cool.

11. These cookies can be made up to three days ahead if stored in a airtight container.

Healthy Fruit Skulls & Bones (K-6)

Ingredients and Supplies

29-ounce canned pear halves (approximately
    7 pears in each can)
Four large bananas
Strawberry ice cream syrup
Black paper plate

Makes 7 healthy servings.

Directions

1. Let the wide end of the pear half represent the skull. The narrow end will be the jaw. Carve out two small holes from the rounded side to represent the skeleton's hollow eyes.

2. Cut a banana in half lengthwise. Lay the halves on the paper plate, crossing them to form an X. Lay the pear on top of the bananas, rounded side up.

3. Drizzle strawberry ice cream syrup over the skull to represent blood.

Simple Bite-Size Cheese Skulls (K-6)

Ingredients and Supplies

10-ounce block of cheddar cheese
Skeleton toothpicks
Round crackers

Makes 15 servings.

Directions

1. Cut cheese into 1-inch cubes.

2. Spear each cube kabob style on a Halloween toothpick featuring a skull shape.

3. Serve on a round cracker.

   Tip: Skeleton toothpicks can only be found at Halloween time. Look for them at discount stores.

Ingredients for Skeleton Treats

CreamyTombstone Dessert (K-6)

4 ounces butter or margarine
  (one stick)
2 1/4 cups cookie crumbs
1/2 cup sugar
One 8-ounce package of cream
  cheese, softened
One 12-ounce whipped topping,
  thawed
2 1/2 cups water
One package (8 serving size)
  gelatin dessert
Rectangular shaped sandwich
  cookies
Decorating icing (various colors)
Decorating bag
Decorating tip #2
Candy corns
Candy pumpkins
This recipe makes 15 servings.

Skeleton Cupcake (K-6)

Cake mix (any flavor)
One 16-ounce canned white frosting
One 16-ounce canned chocolate
  frosting
Grey poster board
Black permanent marker
Decorating bag
Decorating tip #4
Makes approximately 24-28
  cupcakes.

Skeleton Cookies (K-6)

Four large egg whites
1 3/4 cups sugar
1/2 teaspoon grated orange peel
1/2 teaspoon baking powder
1 1/2 cups finely chopped, salted,
  roasted almond
1 3/4 cups flour
Plastic wrap
Bakers Joy®
This recipe makes about 30 cookies.

Healthy Fruit Skulls & Bones (K-6)

29-ounce canned pear halves
  (approximately 7 pears
  in each can)
Four large bananas
Strawberry ice cream syrup
Black paper plate
Makes 7 healthy servings.

Simple Bite-Size Cheese Skulls (K-6)

10-ounce block of cheddar cheese
Skeleton toothpicks
Round crackers
Makes 15 servings.

Spider Treats

Spider Web Rice Krispies Treats® (K-6)

Ingredients and Supplies

One Kellogg's® Rice Krispies Treats® recipe
Twelve black paper plates
Twelve large black gumdrops
96 inches of black string licorice (8 inches per spider)
Red decorating icing (fine tip)
Toothpick

Makes 12 large spider web treats.

Directions

1. Follow the directions on the box of Kellogg's® Rice Krispies® cereal, and make one pan of Rice Krispies Treats®, using slightly more marshmallows than the recipe calls for.

2. Cut the Rice Krispies® mixture into squares. Immediately pull each square apart so it looks like a web.

3. Lay each web on a black paper plate.

4. To make the spider, use a gumdrop for the body, eight 1-inch lengths of licorice for the legs. Push the leg's into the gumdrop with a toothpick. The spider can be made ahead of time, then placed on the still sticky web.

5. Using red decorator icing, dot two eyes on the gumdrop.

Creepy Crawling Spiders (K-6)

Ingredients and Supplies

1 teaspoon peanut butter
Two round crackers
Eight pretzel sticks
Red decorating gel (small tube)

Multiply the amount of peanut butter, crackers, and pretzels by the number of "spiders" to be made.

Directions

1. Spread the peanut butter on one of the round crackers.

2. Arrange pretzel sticks on the cracker to look like spider legs.

3. Add another dab of peanut butter on top of the pretzels, then cover with the second cracker.

4. Add two small dots of red frosting on the top of the cracker for eyes.

161

Oreo® Spiders (K-6)

Ingredients and Supplies

One Oreo® chocolate sandwich cookie
16 inches of black string licorice (cut into eight
   2-inch pieces)
White decorating icing (fine tip)
Two cinnamon imperials

Makes 1 spider

Directions

1. Open up the cookie without breaking the top or bottom halves. Lay four pieces of black string licorice across the white creme filling.

2. Put the cookie back together.

3. Place two tiny dabs of icing on the cookie. Then add a cinnamon candy on top of each dab for eyes.

Spider Web Cookies (K-6)

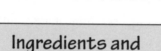

Ingredients and Supplies

Round 3-inch sugar cookies
   (one per student; homemade
   or store bought)

Glaze:
2 cups powdered sugar
4 teaspoons light corn syrup
4 - 6 teaspoons milk

$1/2$ - 1 tablespoon cocoa powder

Makes about 2/3 cup.

Piping frosting:
$1/3$ cup semi-sweet chocolate
1 teaspoon butter
Decorating bag
Decorating tip #2 or #3

Makes about 1/3 cup.

Directions

To make the glaze:

1. Blend the sugar, corn syrup, cocoa, and 3 teaspoons of milk.

2. Of the remaining milk, add 1 teaspoon at a time and keep blending until it is a very smooth consistency. Do not make the glaze until you are ready to use it.

To decorate the cookie:

1. Spread the glaze on top of each cookie quickly. Keep the bowl containing the glaze covered with a damp towel as you are working so that the glaze doesn't dry out.

2. Make the piping frosting at this time, while the glaze hardens on the cookies.

3. Melt the chocolate chips and butter slowly on a low setting in the microwave or over low heat on the stove. Stir with a spoon until the mixture is smooth and creamy. Cool slightly. Do not overcook it.

4. Put the frosting into a decorating bag fitted with a #2 or #3 tip. Use it immediately, this mixture cannot be reheated. Do not double the recipe unless there are two people working together.

5. Pipe a spider web on the cookie. To make the web, pipe three to five concentric circles onto the cookie. Gently pull a toothpick through the frosting starting at the center of each cookie and drawing outward. Do this a few times on each cookie.

Spider Popcorn Balls (K-6)

Ingredients and supplies

4 ounces butter or margarine (one stick)
$1/2$ cup light corn syrup
1 cup sugar
1 teaspoon baking soda
13 cups popped popcorn
Black licorice
Toothpick
2 black jelly beans

Makes 12 spider balls

Directions

1. Mix the butter, corn syrup, and sugar in a saucepan, bringing the mixture to a boil. Let it boil for about three minutes.

2. Add the baking soda and stir. Mixture will get foamy.

3. Mix immediately with the popcorn.

4. Shape into round balls quickly.

5. Attach the black licorice for the leg's while the ball's are still warm, using a toothpick if needed. Attach jelly beans for eyes.

   Tip: Spread softened butter on your hands first- it keeps the popcorn from sticking to them.

Spider Caramel Apple (K-6)

Ingredients and Supplies

Store-bought caramel apple (one per child)
Decorating bag
Decorating tip #2
Optional: plastic spider

Piping frosting
$1/3$ cup semi-sweet chocolate chips and
1 teaspoon butter

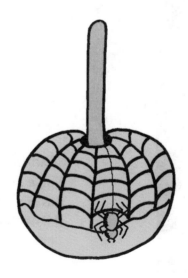

Directions

1. Follow the directions for making chocolate piping frosting in the recipe "Spider Web Cookies" page 162.

2. Pipe a spider web around the caramel apples, working quickly.

   Optional: Attach a plastic spider to the web with a dab of frosting.

Ingredients for Spider Treats

Spider Web Rice Krispies Treats® (K-6)

One Kellogg's® Rice Krispies Treats® recipe
Twelve black paper plates
Twelve large black gumdrops
96 inches of black string licorice (8 inches per spider)
Red decorating icing (with a fine tip)
Toothpick
Makes 12 large spider web treats.

Creepy Crawling Spiders (K-6)

1 teaspoon peanut butter
Two round crackers
Eight pretzel sticks
Red decorating gel (small tube)
Multiply the amount of peanut butter, crackers, and pretzels by the number of "spiders" to be made.

Oreo® Spiders (K-6)

One Oreo® chocolate sandwich cookie
16 inches of black string licorice (cut into eight 2-inch pieces)
White decorating icing (fine tip)
Two cinnamon imperials
Makes 1 spider.

Spider Web Cookies (K-6)

Round 3-inch sugar cookies (one per student; homemade or store bought)

Glaze:

2 cups powdered sugar
4 teaspoons light corn syrup
4-6 teaspoons milk
1/2 - 1 tablespoon cocoa powder
Makes about 2/3 cup.

Piping frosting:

1/3 cup semi-sweet chocolate
1 teaspoon butter
Decorating bag
Decorating tip #2 or #3
Makes about 1/3 cup.

Spider Popcorn Balls (K-6)

4 ounces butter or margarine (one stick)
1/2 cup light corn syrup
1 cup sugar
1 teaspoon baking soda
13 cups popped popcorn
Black licorice
Toothpick
2 black jelly beans
Makes 12 spider balls

Spider Caramel Apple (K-6)

Store-bought caramel apple (one per child)
Decorating bag
Decorating tip #2
Optional: plastic spider

Piping frosting

1/3 cup semi-sweet chocolate chips and 1 teaspoon butter

Witch Treats

Licorice Broomsticks (K-6)

Ingredients

One black licorice vine (broom handle)
36 inches of red string licorice (broom bristles)

Makes 1 broomstick. Multiply the ingredients by the number to be made.

Directions

1. Cut 6 inches off the red licorice and set aside.
2. Fold the 30-inch piece of red string licorice in half. Then fold it in half again, and then again one last time. That's a total of 3 folds.
3. Attach the red folded licorice to the bottom of the black licorice, taking the 6-inch piece and winding it around the red and black licorice until the bundle feels secure (about 4-6 times around). Tie it in a knot and tuck the ends in.
4. Cut the bottoms of the red loops open to resemble broom bristles.

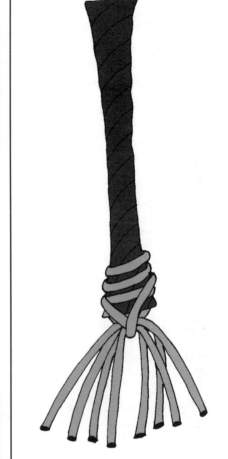

Witch Ice Cream (K-6)

Ingredients

Chocolate flavored sugar cone
One large (3 1/4-inch diameter) round chocolate cookie
2 tablespoons canned chocolate frosting
Large scoop of green sherbet
54 inches of black string licorice (per student)
Two M&Ms®
One candy corn
3-inch piece of red string licorice

Multiply the ingredients by the number to be served.

Directions

1. Center the sugar cone on the rounded side of the cookie with frosting. Let it harden. This will be the witch's hat.
2. Place a large scoop of green sherbet on a plate.
3. Cut the string licorice into nine 6-inch lengths. Push these into the top of the sherbet to represent hair.
4. Attach the hat to the top of the ice cream. Push slightly, piping the underside with frosting if necessary.
5. Decorate the ice cream face. M&Ms® for the eyes, candy corn for the nose, and the red licorice piece for the mouth.
6. Serve immediately

Mini Witches' Hats (K-6)

Ingredients

Box of Bugles® Corn Snacks
Peanut butter
Small bag of mini chocolate chips

Directions

1. Over-fill a bugle (witch's hat) with peanut butter leaving a lump of peanut butter below the edge of the bugle for the witch's face.

2. Attach two mini chocolate chips for eyes.

3. Place four to six mini witches on each plate.

4. Garnish the plate with mini chocolate chips.

   Note: One box of Bugles® Corn Snacks has approximately 230 bugles.

Witches' Flying Broom Cookies (K-6)

Ingredients

1/2 cup packed brown sugar
4 ounces softened butter or margarine (one stick)
2 tablespoons water
1 teaspoon vanilla
1 1/2 cups all-purpose flour
1/4 teaspoon salt

Pretzel rods cut to 5-inch lengths
2 teaspoons shortening
2/3 cup semi-sweet chocolate chips
1/3 cup butterscotch chips

This recipe makes 20 brooms.

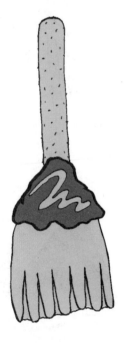

Directions

1. Preheat the oven to 350° F.

2. In a mixer bowl beat the brown sugar, butter, water, and vanilla until creamy (about 3 minutes).

3. Add the flour and salt, beating slowly just enough to mix it all together.

4. Divide the dough into 20 round balls, each about 1 1/4-inch diameter.

5. Place the pretzel rods on the un-greased cookie sheets. About five to six will fit comfortably.

6. Place one ball of cookie dough at the end of each pretzel. Press the dough down slightly with your fingers so it attaches to the pretzel. Then press the cookie dough with a fork to make tine marks that will represent broom straw.

7. Bake about 10-12 minutes. Do not overcook. You will want the cookies to be firm but not brown.

8. Remove the cookies from the oven and cool them on a wire rack.

9. Put the brooms on wax paper.

10. Melt the shortening and chocolate chips in a microwave oven at a low setting or over low heat on your stove. Do not overcook. Stir until smooth and creamy.

11. Spoon the melted chip mixture over each cookie where the cookie and pretzel connect.

12. Melt the butterscotch chips at a low setting in the microwave oven or over low heat on your stove. Stir until smooth and creamy. Drizzle over the chocolate area.

13. Leave the cookies on the wax paper for a few hours to let the chocolate dry.

Bewitching Hats (K-6)

Ingredients

Thirty-two chocolate Hershey Kisses® (unwrapped)
One 11¹/2-ounce package fudge striped   short-
   bread cookies
Red decorating icing (fine tip)

This recipe makes 32 servings.

Directions

1. Turn the fudge cookie upside down so the flat side is up. Squirt some icing onto the center of the cookie.

2. Place the flat bottom of the chocolate kiss on the frosted part to form the peak of the witch's hat.

3. Pipe icing and a bow around the kiss to represent a hat band.

Rice Cake Witches (K-6)

Ingredients and Supplies

Twenty-eight large rice cakes
   (one per student)
One 16-ounce canned vanilla
   frosting
One 16-ounce canned chocolate
   frosting
Green food coloring

Black construction paper
Twenty-eight candy corns
Fifty-six M&Ms®
Decorating bag
Decorating tip #3 or #4

Makes 28 rice cake witches.

Directions

1. For quick green frosting add green food coloring to vanilla frosting. Mix until well blended.

2. Ice the rice cake with green frosting.

3. With chocolate frosting in your decorating bag, squiggle hair around the top edge of the rice cake.

4. Cut out a peaked witch's hat from the construction paper. Attach it to the top edge of the witch's face.

5. With a dab of frosting, attach the candy corn as a nose and the M&Ms® as eyes.

6. Using the chocolate frosting, make a mouth.

167

Ingredients for Witch Treats

Licorice Broomsticks (K-6)

One black licorice vine
   (broom handle)
36 inches of red string licorice
   (broom bristles)
Makes 1 broomstick. Multiply
   the ingredients by the number
   to be made.

Witch Ice Cream (K-6)

Chocolate flavored sugar cone
One large (3 1/4" diameter) round
   chocolate cookie
2 tablespoons chocolate frosting
Large scoop of green sherbet
54 inches of black string licorice
   (per student)
Two M&Ms®
One candy corn
3-inch piece of red string licorice
Multiply the ingredients by the
   number to be served.

Mini Witches' Hats (K-6)

Box of Bugles® Corn Snacks
Peanut butter
Small bag of mini chocolate chips

Witches' Flying Broom Cookies (K-6)

1/2 cup packed brown sugar
4 ounces softened butter or margarine (one stick)

2 tablespoons water
1 teaspoon vanilla
1 1/2 cups all-purpose flour
1/4 teaspoon salt
Pretzel rods cut to 5-inch lengths
2 teaspoons shortening
2/3 cup semi-sweet chocolate chips
1/3 cup butterscotch chips
This recipe makes 20 brooms.

Bewitching Hats (K-6)

Thirty-two chocolate Hershey
   Kisses® (unwrapped)
One 11 1/2-ounce package fudge
   striped shortbread cookies
Red decorating icing (fine tip)
This recipe makes 32 servings.

Rice Cake Witches (K-6)

Twenty-eight large rice cakes
   (one per student)
One 16-ounce canned vanilla
   frosting
One 16-ounce canned chocolate
   frosting
Green food coloring
Black construction paper
Twenty-eight candy corns
Fifty-six M&Ms®
Decorating bag
Decorating tip #3 or #4
Makes 28 rice cake witches.

Additional Treats

Halloween (Stained Glass) Cookies (K-6)

Ingredients and Supplies

1/2 cup butter or margarine (softened)
1 cup packed brown sugar
One egg
1 teaspoon vanilla
1 1/4 cups all-purpose flour
1/2 teaspoon baking powder
1/2 teaspoon salt
Halloween cookie cutters
Aluminum foil
Hard candy or suckers

Directions

1. Cream the butter, brown sugar, and egg.

2. Add the vanilla.

3. In a separate bowl, mix the flour, baking powder, and salt.

4. Combine the wet and dry ingredients until well mixed.

5. Add extra flour if needed for a creamy consistency.

6. Cover the bowl and refrigerate for a few hours.

7. Lightly flour your work area and roll out a section of dough. Using Halloween cookie cutters, cut your designs out.

8. Put aluminum foil on the cookie sheet. Lightly grease the foil. Place your cookies on the foil.

9. Crush the candy by placing it in a bag and smashing it with a hammer until finely broken.

10. Sprinkle some of the broken candy over each cookie.

11. Bake at 325° F until the candy bubbles. Let the cookies cool before removing them from the pan.

169

Cookie Decorating Center (K-6)

Ingredients and Supplies

Foam meat trays
Cookies
Popsicle sticks or plastic butter knives
3-ounce paper cups
16-ounce canned frosting (any flavor)
Assorted sprinkles and/or colored sugar
Small sandwich bags/ twist ties
Plastic wrap
Option #1: Several colors of frosting
Option #2: Cupcake pans

What did you like about cookie decorating?

Zachariah Fitch age 5
"Doing it was fun!"

Kelly Hill age 6
"I don't know—Icing them!"

Nick Ripple age 11
"I like putting the sprinkles on and eating them."

Directions

1. Lay the cookies onto meat trays.

2. Add to the trays, a popsicle stick, paper cup filled with a small amount of frosting, and a bag of sprinkles or colored sugar.

3. Wrap with plastic wrap.

4. Children get to decorate their own cookie using the popsicle stick to spread their frosting. Let them eat their cookie or take it home.

   Option #1: Give several different colors of frosting, and more than one bag of decorations.

   Option #2: Fill cupcake pans with decorations and frosting to eliminate the foam trays.

Ingredients for Additional Treats

Halloween (Stained glass) cookies (K-6)

1/2 cup butter or margarine (softened)
1 cup packed brown sugar
One egg
1 teaspoon vanilla
1 1/4 cups all-purpose flour
1/2 teaspoon baking powder
1/2 teaspoon salt
Halloween cookie cutters
Aluminum foil
Hard candy or suckers

Cookie Decorating Center (K-6)

Foam meat trays
Cookies
Popsicle sticks or plastic butter knives
3-ounce paper cups
16-ounce canned frosting (any flavor)
Assorted sprinkles and/or colored sugar
Small sandwich bags/ twist ties
Plastic wrap
Option #1: Several Colors of Frosting
Option #2: Cupcake pans

CHAPTER FIVE
Drinks

Helpful Hints for Drinks

To add some uniqueness to your drinks try some of these hair-raising, spine tingling, electrifying helpful hints and enjoy.

1. Serve assorted juices in beakers. A unique idea for a Frankenstein theme.

2. Are you having a witch party? Serve the drinks in a large cast iron Dutch oven or a witch cauldron. Witch cauldrons can be purchased at Halloween time from discount stores.

3. Make broomstick straws to serve with your drinks. Cut a strip of black construction paper 1" x 4". Wrap it around one end of a straw (leaving a $1/2$-inch overhang), glue, let it dry. Fringe the ends with scissors. Serve fringe side end up.

4. Use licorice twists for straws. Cut a small amount off both ends and they are ready for sipping.

5. Cut a small Halloween shape out of poster board and glue it onto the end of a straw. Also, try making a ring shape out of poster board, glue the ring shape to the back of the Halloween shape, let it dry. Slide it onto the straw.

6. Freeze items into ice cubes. Plastic bugs, spiders, raisins, gummy worms, and blueberries work well. However, use extreme caution that children do not swallow these items.

7. Boil water before freezing to make clear ice cubes.

8. Kids will enjoy having vampire eyes (ice) cubes in their juice drink. To make: Half fill cupcake tins with juice. Freeze until slushy (1-2 hours). Push a seedless green grape into the center of each slush mixture, then refreeze until firm. To release: Soak the bottom of the pan in warm water for a few seconds then turn the pan upside down onto a clean towel. If they don't slide out, soak the pan in warm water for a few more seconds. The eyes should pop out. Put one or two eyes in each glass then fill with more juice.

9. Add a frozen hand to your punch. Fill a surgical glove (powderless, purchase at grocery stores) with water. Add food coloring if desired. Twist tie the end. Hang the glove in your freezer from a shelf, allow it to freeze overnight. Before serving cut the glove off and place the hand into the punch bowl. Gelatin dessert can also be used in place of water and food coloring.

10. Pumpkin faces can be made by pushing whole cloves into oranges to make the facial features of jack-o-lanterns. Place the pumpkins into a punchbowl.

11. Use a fresh large pumpkin as a punchbowl. Remove and clean the pumpkins' insides. Refrigerate until ready to use. Draw a face on the pumpkin with paints or markers. Add your drink to the pumpkin and serve.

12. Use dry ice (solid carbon dioxide) to get that eerie fogging effect that's fun to have at Halloween time. You may purchase dry ice from most grocery stores, ice cream shops, or meat stores. Most places request you order the dry ice ahead of time (1-3 weeks) and pick it up on the day of the party. Dry ice is sold in blocks. A small block (3-5 pounds) is plenty for a classroom party. The ice can be chopped into smaller pieces if needed. Dry ice must be handled with gloves because it can burn your skin. Tongs will work. Dry ice is wrapped in paper when you purchase it. To activate the ice, place it in a container with warm water. Steam will start immediately and will surround the container and rise up and out. As water cools, ice will form around the dry ice, causing it to stop bubbling. Salt water can cause the action to last longer. After fif-

174

teen minutes, drain the cold water from the container and replace it with warm water to start the reaction again. A fan can be used aimed at the fog to help direct it, if needed. Dry ice can be added to your punch if it's in a punch bowl but be careful that no pieces end up in anybodies drink when serving. Consider wrapping the ice with cheesecloth.

13. Serve drinks in oranges which are carved and used for cups. You will need two oranges, one slightly smaller than the other. Cut a small section off the top of both oranges and scoop out the insides exactly like you do for a pumpkin. Turn the smaller pumpkin inside out and slide it into the large orange. You have lined the orange and are now ready to serve your beverage in it. Garnish with carved kumquats (a small fruit that looks like a pumpkin).

14. Carve a jack-o-lantern face into a kumquat. Stick the kumquat onto a toothpick and use for garnish.

15. Last but not least, garnish, drinks with fruit. Maraschino cherries, pineapples, strawberries, raspberries, apples, oranges and melon slices all work well for children's drinks. Colored straws are a favorite too.

Cheers!

Drinks

All recipes make at least: Twenty-eight 1-cup servings, Thirty-seven 3/4-cup servings, Fifty-six 1/2-cup servings

Bat Brew (K-6)

Ingredients

Two 12-ounce cans frozen grape juice (diluted with six cans of water)

One 2-liter bottle of gingerale
Half gallon of lime sherbet

Most fourth through sixth graders will drink 1 cup or more of punch. Younger children, second through third grade, need 3/4 cup. Kindergarten through first grade will drink 1/2 cup.

Directions

1. Thaw the grape juice and pour it into a large punch bowl.
2. Dilute with 72 ounces (six cans) of water.
3. Add the gingerale, and stir.
4. Five minutes before serving add sherbet and stir.

Cat Punch (K-6)

Ingredients

One 8-ounce bottle lemon juice
Three 64-ounce bottles of apple juice

One 12-ounce can frozen orange juice (dilute with three cans of water)
4 apples (cut for garnish)

Directions

1. Mix all ingredients together in a punch bowl.
2. Stir well, garnish with apple slices.

Frankensteins Favorite Shake (K-6)

Ingredients and Supplies

10 cups frozen blueberries
5 cups applesauce
5 cups plain yogurt
8 cups milk
3 tablespoons granulated sugar
Tall clear glasses
Straws

Directions

1. Puree ingredients in a blender, food processor or mixer to make a purple colored shake .

2. Serve in clear glasses with straws.

Spooky Ghost Milk (K-6)

Ingredients and Supplies

1¹/₂ gallons milk
Ten large sized bananas (two sliced for garnish)
Toothpicks

Directions

1. Blend milk and bananas until only slightly chunky.

2. Garnish with bananas

Jack-O-Lantern Juice (K-6)

Ingredients

Three 12-ounce cans frozen orange juice (dilute with nine cans of water)
10 cups of gingerale

Directions

1. Mix all ingredients together in a punch bowl.

2. Thats all! Cheers!

Rattling Bone Brew (K-6)

Ingredients and Supplies

Four 2-liter bottles of gingerale
Blueberries (two per child)
Round ice cube trays

Directions

1. Freeze blueberries in trays to form skeleton eyes. Make these the day before.

2. Serve gingerale with skeleton eyes.

Spider Cider (K-6)

Ingredients and Supplies

Three 64-ounce bottles apple cider
One 32-ounce bottle apple cider
Clear plastic cups
Black permanent ink marker

Directions

1. Draw a spider on the outside bottom of each cup. Add cider.

2. Pour the cider, serve it, and listen for giggles and shrieks.

Witch's Bubbling Brew (K-6)

Ingredients and Supplies

Four 2-liter bottles clear soda pop
Blue food coloring
Colored straws
Fruit (for garnish)

Directions

1. Add a few drops of food coloring to each bottle of soda. Put the bottle cap back on and shake the soda.

2. Serve immediately in clear cups with colored straws and garnish with fruit.

Ingredients for Drinks

Bat Brew (K-6)

Two 12-ounce cans frozen
   grape juice (diluted with
   six cans of water)
One 2-liter bottle of gingerale
Half gallon of lime sherbet

Cat Punch (K-6)

One 8-ounce bottle lemon juice
Three 64-ounce bottles of
   apple juice
One 12-ounce can frozen
   orange juice (dilute with
   three cans of water)
4 apples (cut for garnish)

Frankensteins Favorite
Shake (K-6)

10 cups frozen blueberries
5 cups applesauce
5 cups plain yogurt
8 cups milk
3 tablespoons granulated sugar
Tall clear glasses
Straws

Spooky Ghost Milk (K-6)

1½ gallons milk
Ten large sized bananas (two sliced
   for garnish)
Toothpicks

Jack-O-Lantern Juice (K-6)

Three 12-ounce cans frozen
   orange juice (dilute with nine
   cans of water)
10 cups of gingerale

Rattling Bone Brew (K-6)

Four 2-liter bottles of gingerale
Blueberries (two per child)
Round ice cube trays

Spider Cider (K-6)

Three 64-ounce bottles apple cider
One 32-ounce bottle apple cider
Clear plastic cups
Black permanent ink marker

Witch's Bubbling Brew (K-6)

Four 2-liter bottles clear soda pop
Blue food coloring
Colored straws
Fruit (for garnish)

CHAPTER SIX
Quick and Easy
Parent Costumes

Helpful Hints for Parent Costumes

1. Add character to your costumes with face paints.

2. Any of these costumes can be spiced up using items from craft and fabric stores. Start with glitter, beads, and felt. Let your imagination and time dictate what and how to do it.

3. To make your head look square for the Frankenstein costume, choose one of the following methods:

   1 Paint a small cardboard box black, and fit snugly over the top of your head.

   2. If your hair is short, tease and spray your hair to stand up in a square shape.

   3. Cut off the top half of a gallon plastic milk container. Paint it black, and fit it over the top of your head.

4. Special effects can be achieved for your ghost costume by adding a plastic ball & chain (purchase at costume stores or use old toys).

5. To attach spider legs use one of the following methods:

   1. Tuck the waist band of nylons into the top of your pants.

   2. Cut off the panty part of the nylons and glue the legs spread evenly to the underside of a black belt. Hook the belt onto your waist.

6. If you would like to spice up your witch costume add plastic spiders and other creatures to your cape and shoulder area. You may also add stars made out of glitter, felt and puff paints. Purchase a plastic crooked nose at a costume store. Kids love the authentic look.

7. Check the following chart. It can help find items that are needed for costumes in this chapter.

Discount Stores	Craft Stores	Costume Stores	Department Stores
Bat mask	Fiberfill	Bat mask	Bat mask
Cat whiskers	Pumpkin leaf bags	Cat whiskers	Cat whiskers
Fiberfill	Fabric paints	Pumpkin leaf bags	Pumpkin leaf bags
Shoulder pads	Witch hats	Witch hats	Witch hats
Witch hats	Witch brooms	Witch brooms	Witch brooms
Witch brooms	Black fingernail polish	Black fingernail polish	
Black fingernail polish			

Fabric Stores	Grocery Stores	Thrift Stores	Hardware Stores
Fiberfill	Witch hats	Witch hats	Pumpkin leaf bags
Shoulder pads	Black fingernail polish	Witch brooms	
Fabric paint			

180

Bat

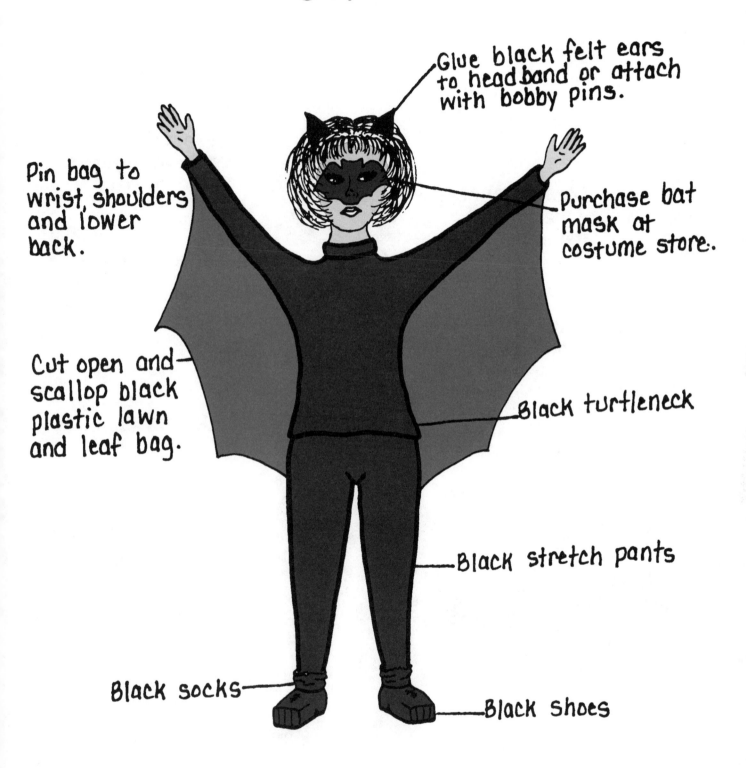

Glue black felt ears to head band or attach with bobby pins.

Pin bag to wrist, shoulders and lower back.

Purchase bat mask at costume store.

Cut open and scallop black plastic lawn and leaf bag.

Black turtleneck

Black stretch pants

Black socks

Black shoes

Cat

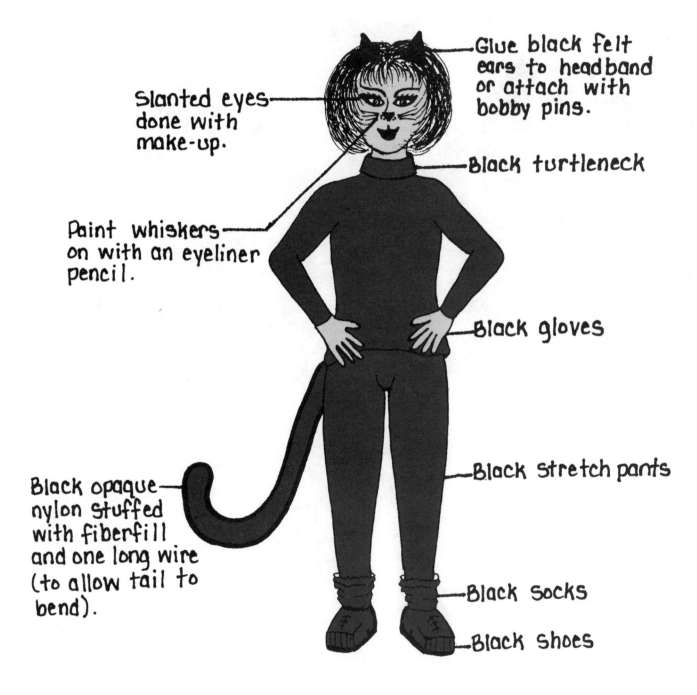

Glue black felt ears to headband or attach with bobby pins.

Slanted eyes done with make-up.

Paint whiskers on with an eyeliner pencil.

Black turtleneck

Black gloves

Black opaque nylon stuffed with fiberfill and one long wire (to allow tail to bend).

Black stretch pants

Black socks

Black shoes

Frankenstein

Thick shoulder pads

Bolts (corks painted gray) attached to wire that hooks to neck from behind.

Black or green oversized jacket

If possible, match color of the pants to the jacket.

Cut jagged

Embarrassing socks!

Black shoes

* Check helpful hints for parent costumes for ways to make your head look square.

Ghost

Cut eye openings.

Cut slits for arms.

White Sheet
(How tall are you?
Double that
length and add
approximately
12" extra for
sheet size.)

white tights

White socks

White shoes

Pumpkin

Green felt stem

Round circle of orange felt (slit and overlapped to fit head). May glue to a headband.

Gather neckline with yarn until comfortable.

Make slits for armholes.

Pumpkin leaf bag (the kind sold at Halloween)

Cut open bottom of bag.

Black tights

Black shoes

Skeleton

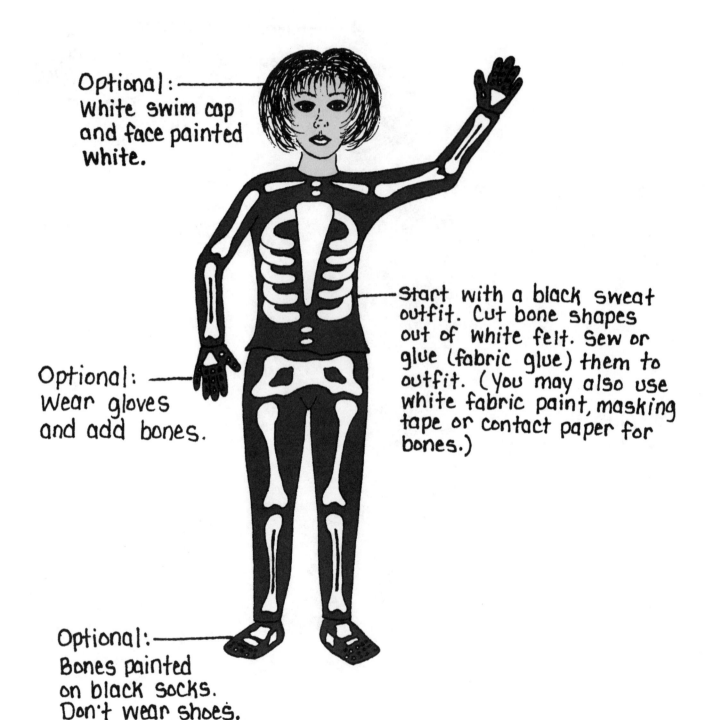

Optional:
White swim cap
and face painted
white.

Optional:
Wear gloves
and add bones.

Start with a black sweat
outfit. Cut bone shapes
out of white felt. Sew or
glue (fabric glue) them to
outfit. (You may also use
white fabric paint, masking
tape or contact paper for
bones.)

Optional:
Bones painted
on black socks.
Don't wear shoes.

Spider

Paint a spider web with white fabric paint.

Black turtleneck

To make spider legs, use three pairs of black opaque nylons stuffed with fiberfill and wire (allows bending.)

Black stretch pants

Black shoes

Black socks

* Check helpful hints for parent costumes for ways to attach legs.

Witch

Store bought witch hat

Ratty, wild looking hair

Black dress and shawl

Fake long fingernails, polished black

Witch broom

Black nylons

Black boots

★ Check helpful hints for parent costumes if you would like to spice up the outfit.

Final Thoughts

You can finally take a breath.

The bell has rung.

The kids are leaving.

Did it go like you planned?

Maybe or maybe not.

But did the kids have fun?

You bet they did!

Till next time.

Willie

Share your ideas and/or suggestions for future
***What Do I Do?*™ books.**

Wilhelminia Ripple
Oakbrook Publishing House
P.O. Box 2463
Littleton, CO 80161-2463

INDEX

190

Order Form

Become an expert the easy way! Order your copies of *Halloween School Parties: What Do I Do?*™ and *Valentine School Parties: What Do I Do?*™

Use our toll free hotline to order today, call **1-888-738-1733**

Oakbrook Publishing House
P.O. Box 2463
Littleton, CO 80161-2463
(303) 738-1733
FAX: (303) 797-1995

Send To: Name: _____

Address: _____

City, State & Zip Code: _____

Phone: (_____)_____

Book Title	Quantity	Price	Total
Halloween School Parties: What Do I Do?™ ISBN: 0-9649939-8-8	_____	**$19.95** ea.	_____
Valentine School Parties: What Do I Do?™ ISBN: 0-9649939-9-6	_____	**$17.95** ea.	_____
		Sub-total	_____
		Shipping & Handling (see below)	_____
		Colorado Res. add 3.8% sales tax	_____
		Total	_____

Check or Money Order _____ payable to: Oakbrook Publishing House

Credit Card _____   VISA _____ Master Card _____ Discover _____

Card Number _____ Exp.Date_____

Signature _____

Canadian orders must be accompanied by a postal money order in U.S. funds.

Shipping and Handling charges are: 1st class $3.50, 4th class $2.25
(Allow 7-10 days for 4th class mail), additional books add $1.00 each.

Please note: The index is on the opposite side.
Please photocopy this page and pass along to your friends.